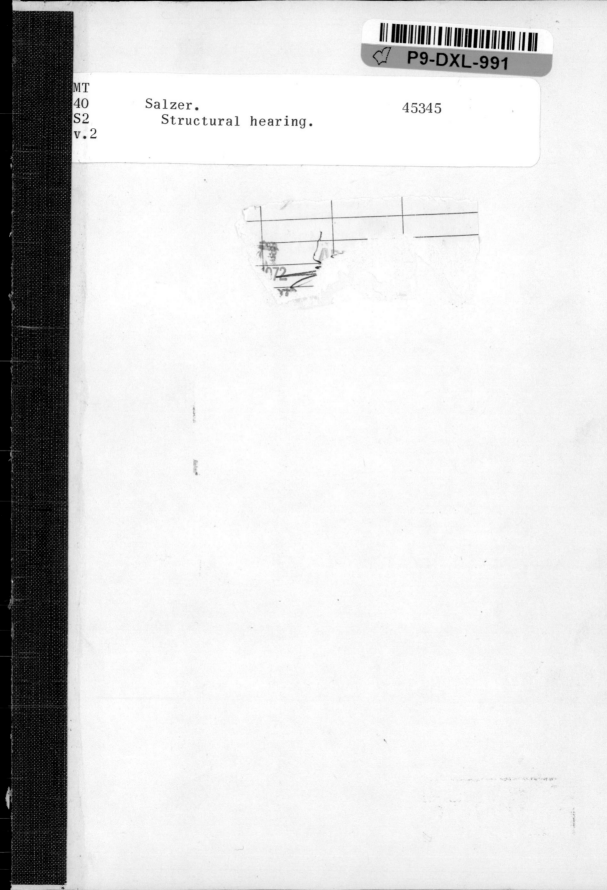

Structural Hearing

TONAL COHERENCE IN MUSIC

Structural Hearing

TONAL COHERENCE IN MUSIC

VOLUME TWO

BY FELIX SALZER

WITH A FOREWORD BY LEOPOLD MANNES

Charles Boni, NEW YORK, NINETEEN FIFTY-TWO

Published by Charles Boni
3 Grove Court, New York 14, N. Y.

Acknowledgments

Grateful acknowledgment is made to the following publishers for permission to use
    copyrighted material:
Associated Music Publishers, Inc. (Ex. X, 410, 411, 445, 453).
Boosey & Hawkes, Inc. (Ex. 239, 241, 377, 386, 406, 407, 412, 416, 419, 452).
Elkan-Vogel Co., Inc. for Durand et Cie. (Ex. 290).
Leeds Music Corp. (Ex. 380, 451).
E. B. Marks Music Corp. (Ex. 413).
Oxford University Press, Ltd. (Ex. 319, 331).
Salabert, Inc. (Ex. 414).

I wish, furthermore, to thank the following for permission to reprint material from their
    publications:
Harvard University Press, for various quotations from *Historical Anthology of Music;
    Oriental, Medieval and Renaissance*, Vol. I, Revised edition, 1949 (Ex. 184, 185, 510,
    513, 515, 524, 525).
E. B. Marks Music Corp. for Ex. 415.
Oxford University Press, Ltd. for Ex. 209.
G. Schirmer, Inc. for Ex. 418 and for the excerpts from Ruth and Thomas Martin's
    translation of *The Magic Flute* (Ex. 483).

F.S.

Contents

Notes to the Reader   vi
List of Musical Illustrations   vii
Notes and Glossary for the Voice-Leading Graphs   xiii
List of Sources (Abbreviations)   xv

Musical Illustrations

	Ex. Nos.	Pages
Part I		
Chapter Two	I–X	2–7
Part II		
Chapter Two	1–11	8–11
Chapter Three	12–95	12–27
Chapter Four	96–117	27–29
Chapter Five	118–268	30–89
Chapter Six	269–400	90–164
Chapter Seven	401–472	165–237
Chapter Eight	473–507	238–311
Part III		
Chapter One	508–509	312–314
Chapter Two	510–539	314–349

Notes to the Reader

Ideally, a book of this type would present every musical quotation discussed, along with its voice-leading graphs. This proved impractical for reasons of space; therefore, the following plan has been adopted. With very few exceptions the examples in Part I, Part II through Chapter Six and in Part III appear in complete form (music and graphs). In Chapter Seven the music has been omitted for most quotations from standard literature and for the quotations of large excerpts. Chapter Eight, which deals with complete compositions, offers exclusively voice-leading graphs without the music. Since all the music omitted is from available editions, it is hoped that this procedure will not be disadvantageous to the reader.

It has been found practical to print many examples and their graphs (especially the larger ones) running across facing pages, in order to make the course of voice leading clearer for the eye, and to avoid awkward turning of pages as much as possible. The first such example is Ex. X. If there is doubt about the continuity, the reader is advised to orient himself by means of the measure numbers.

In the quotations from music of earlier times, treble and bass clefs have been consistently used, even if the transcriptions in the indicated sources do not follow this procedure. Furthermore, in some compositions, transpositions and change of note-values have been carried out, thus reverting to the readings of earlier sources.

List of Musical Illustrations

Example number

Adam de La Halle

Monophonic Ballade: Li maus
d'amer, 524
Rondeau: Tant con je vivrai, 525

Anonymous Composer

Alleluia Angelus Domini, 510
Allemande, 447
Basse Danse, 268
Benedicamus Domino (School
of St. Martial), 511
Benedicat ergo (School of
Compostela), 512
Folk Tune, 8, 215
Motets of the Thirteenth Cen-
tury, 517, 518, 519, 520,
521, 522, 526, 527
Rondeau: Amours et ma dame
aussi, 523
Viderunt Hemanuel (School
of St. Martial), 513

Bach, C. P. E.

Fantasia, 224
Minuetto, 154

Bach, J. S.

Aria variata, Variation 9, 232
Brandenburg Concerto No. 1
—2nd movement, 240
Cantata: Du wahrer Gott und
Davids Sohn, 424
Chorales:
No. 5, 276, 392
No. 6, 1
No. 7, 11

Example number

No. 11, 160
No. 23, III
No. 24, 168
No. 42, 182
Peters No. 43, 237
No. 55, 312
No. 64, 236
No. 88, 120
No. 110, 179
Peters No. 118, 177
No. 166, 347
No. 167, 348
No. 177, 313
No. 192, 269
No. 229, 321
No. 233, 174
No. 246, 123
No. 280, 328
No. 294, II
No. 320, 327
No. 330, 140
No. 337, 119
No. 346, 145
No. 348, 122
No. 361, 339
No. 362, 176
No. 366, 162
No. 367, 163, 175
Courante (Partita No. 5), 200
Courante (Suite pour le cla-
vecin, E♭ Major), 228
Fugue No. 5 (Well-Tem-
pered Clavier, Bk I), 474
Gavotte (French Suite No. 5), 132

Example number

Little Prelude, C minor,   147
Little Prelude, C minor,   249
Little Prelude, F Major,   170
Little Prelude, G minor,   493
Minuet 2 (Partita No. 1),   495
Praeambulum (Partita No. 5),   231
Praeludium (Partita No. 1),   225
Prelude No. 1 (Well-Tem-
    pered Clavier, Bk I),   152
Prelude No. 6 (Well-Tem-
    pered Clavier, Bk I),   158
Prelude No. 10 (Well-Tem-
    pered Clavier, Bk I),   246
Prelude No. 21 (Well-Tem-
    pered Clavier, Bk I),   I
Prelude No. 2 (Well-Tem-
    pered Clavier, Bk II),   169
Prelude No. 7 (Well-Tem-
    pered Clavier, Bk II),   280

Bartók
Bagatelle, Op 6, No. 4,   418
Bourrée (Mikrokosmos),   504
From 10 Easy Pieces for Piano,   441
Piano Concerto No. 3—1st
    movement,   480
Piano Pieces for Children, No.
    32,   186
String Quartet No. 5—2nd
    movement,   452
Ukrainian Song (Petite Suite),   241

Beethoven
Bagatelle, Op 119, No. 11,   3
Piano Concerto, G Major, No. 4
    —1st movement,   420
Piano Sonata, F minor, Op 2,
    No. 1—2nd movement,   442
    —3rd movement,   206
Piano Sonata, A Major, Op 2,
    No. 2—2nd movement,   10
Piano Sonata, C Major, Op 2,
    No. 3—4th movement,   298
Piano Sonata, C minor, Op 10,
    No. 1—1st movement,   463

Example number

—2nd movement,   443
Piano Sonata, D Major, Op 10,
    No. 3—1st movement,   458
Piano Sonata, C minor, Op 13
    —2nd movement,   383
Piano Sonata, E Major, Op 14,
    No. 1—2nd movement,   265
    —3rd movement,   229
Piano Sonata, G Major, Op 14,
    No. 2—1st movement,   254
Piano Sonata, Bb Major, Op 22
    —1st movement,   461
Piano Sonata, C♯ minor, Op
    27, No. 2—1st movement,   375
Piano Sonata, G Major, Op 31,
    No. 1—1st movement,   440
Piano Sonata, Eb Major, Op 31,
    No. 3—1st movement,   288
Piano Sonata, C Major, Op 53
    —Introduzione,   430
Piano Sonata, F minor, Op 57
    —1st movement,   464
Piano Sonata, G Major, Op 79
    —1st movement,   226
Piano Sonata, Eb Major, Op
    81a—1st movement,   289
Piano Sonata, E minor, Op 90
    —1st movement,   450
Piano Sonata, E Major, Op 109,
    —1st movement,   221
String Quartet, Op 18, No. 5
    —3rd movement,   491
Symphony No. 7—1st
    movement,   462
Symphony No. 9—3rd
    movement,   222

Bizet
Carmen: Seguidilla (Act I),   408

Brahms
Feldeinsamkeit,   485
Intermezzo, Op 118, No. 2,   308
Intermezzo, Op 119, No. 1,   477

Example number

Piano Sonata, F minor, Op 5
  —1st movement,   133
Sextet No. 2, Op 36—1st movement,   454
Symphony No. 3—1st move-
  ment,   503
Waltz, Op 39, No. 8,   494

Byrd
Pavane: The Earle of Salis-
  bury,   243, 490
Sacerdotes Domini,   427

Carissimi
Cantata: Mary Stuart,   209

Chopin
Etude, Op 10, No. 4,   283
Etude, Op 25, No. 5,   251
Mazurka, Op 6, No. 1,   362
Mazurka, Op 7, No. 2,   361
Mazurka, Op 17, No. 2,   304, 499
Mazurka, Op 17, No. 4   359
Mazurka, Op 24, No. 3,   285, 350
Mazurka, Op 30, No. 4,   357
Mazurka, Op 41, No. 4,   250
Mazurka, Op 59, No. 2,   311, 432
Mazurka, Op 63, No. 2,   284
Mazurka, Op 68, No. 2
  (Posth.),   315
Mazurka, Op. 68, No. 4
  (Posth.),   387
Nocturne, Op 9, No. 2,   324, 500
Nocturne, Op 27, No. 1,   378
Nocturne, Op 27, No. 2,   506
Nocturne, Op 32, No. 1,   216
Nocturne, Op 37, No. 2,   508
Nocturne, Op 48, No. 2,   456
Polonaise, Op 26,   431
Polonaise, Op 40,   433
Polonaise-Fantasy,   409
Prelude, Op 28, No. 1,   492
Waltz, Op 34, No. 2,   131
Waltz, Op 64, No. 2,   297, 393
Waltz, Op 69, No. 2,   155

Example number

Waltz, E Major (Posth.),   142

Clementi
Sonatina, G Major, Op 36,
  No. 2,   220

Cléreau
Kyrie 1 (Missa: In me transierunt),   274

Copland
Appalachian Spring   239
Piano Sonata—1st movement,   416
3 Excerpts from *Our Town*,
  No. 1,   412

Couperin
La Bandoline,   323
La Favorite,   426

Debussy
Bruyères,   478
Prélude à l'après-midi d'un
  faune,   455

Dowland
Ayre: What if I never speed,   473

Dufay
Rondeau: Adieu m'amour,   536

Dunstable
Chanson: Puisque m'amour,   535
Sub tuam protectionem,   534

Farnaby
A Toye,   435

Fogliano
Lauda: Ave Maria,   185

Franck
Prelude, Aria and Finale,   405

Frescobaldi
Corrente,   484
La Frescobalda,   486

Froberger
Suite: "Auf die Mayerin",   212

Gastoldi
Balletto: Speme amorosa,   403

Example number

Gesualdo
Madrigal: Io pur respiro,   479

Gibbons
The Queene's Command,   271

Handel
Courante (Suite No. 14),   329
Double,   202
Minuet,   238
Variation 1 (Air from Suite
    No. 3),   227

Haydn
Minuet,   7
Piano Sonata, D Major, No. 19
    —2nd movement,   211
Piano Sonata, C Major, No. 21
    —1st movement,   247
Piano Sonata, G Major, No. 27
    —2nd movement,   214
Piano Sonata, F Major, No. 29
    —2nd movement,   390
Piano Sonata, C Major, No. 35
    —1st movement,   210
Piano Sonata, G minor, No. 44
    —2nd movement,   318
Piano Sonata, Eb Major, No.
    52—3rd movement,   272
String Quartet, Op 20, No. 5
    —3rd movement,   401
String Quartet, Op 76, No. 1
    —2nd movement,   349
String Quartet, Op 76, No. 4
    —3rd movement,   336
Symphony, G Major, No. 100
    —4th movement,   266
Symphony, D Major, No. 104
    —1st movement,   459

Hindemith
Interludium (Ludus Tonalis),   489
Piano Sonata No. 1—1st move-
    ment,   453
Piano Sonata No. 2—1st move-
    ment,   505

Example number

—2nd movement,   410
Piano Sonata No. 3—1st move-
    ment,   X

Isaac
Kyrie (Missa Carminum),   538

Josquin Des Prés
Missa: Pange lingua,   156
Motet: Ave Maria,   273
Motet: O Domine Jesu Christe
    (1st part),   539
Motet: Tu pauperum refug-
    ium,   184

Lasso
Christe Dei soboles,   509
Motet: Recordare Jesu pie,   402

Leoninus
Alleluia Pascha,   514

Liszt
Liebestraum (Nocturne No. 3),   300

Machaut
Ballade No. 3,   530
Ballade No. 26,   533
Rondeau No. 13,   531
Virelai No. 31,   532
Virelai No. 32,   529
Virelai No. 38,   528

Mahler
Kindertotenlieder, No. 1,   445
Das Lied von der Erde, No. 6,   386

Marenzio
Madrigal: Io piango,   482

Martinů
Sonata for Cello and Piano No.
    2—2nd movement,   411
Sonata for Violin and Piano
    No. 2—2nd movement,   414

Mendelssohn
A Midsummer Night's Dream,
    Overture,   436

Example number

Song Without Words, Op 62,
No. 1, 205
Song Without Words, Op 102,
No. 2, 218

Monteverdi
Madrigal: Lasciatemi morire, 501

Moussorgsky
Ballet of the Unhatched
Chickens (Pictures from
an Exhibition), 428

Mozart
Courante (Suite, K. 399), 213
Don Giovanni: Aria ("Dalla
sua pace"), 219
—Quartet ("Non ti fidar"), 267
Fantasia, D minor, K. 397, 207
Fantasia, C minor, K. 475, 507
Fugue, C Major (Fantasia, K.
394), 235
The Magic Flute: Aria
("Ach, ich fühl's"), 483
Piano Sonata, C Major, K. 279
—1st movement 444
—3rd movement, 199, 201
Piano Sonata, F Major, K. 280
—1st movement, 198, 217
—2nd movement, 388, 475
Piano Sonata, G Major, K. 283
—1st movement, 244, 248
Piano Sonata, D Major, K. 311
—2nd movement, 183
Piano Sonata, A minor, K. 331
—1st movement, VIII
Piano Sonata, C minor, K. 457
3rd movement, 208
Piano Sonata, C Major, K. 545
—1st movement, 143
—2nd movement, 233
Piano Sonata, D Major, K. 576
—1st movement, 277
Rondo, F Major, K. 494, 332
Rondo, A minor, K. 511, 203

Example number

Trio, E♭ Major, K. 498
—1st movement, 230

Muffat Gottlieb
Air (Suite, B♭ Major), 245

Obrecht
Osanna (Missa: Je ne de-
mande), 537

Peerson
The Primerose, 320

Perotinus
Organum triplum, 516

Perotinus, Style of
Organum, 515

Prokofieff
Gavotte, Op 77, No. 4, 380
Piano Sonata No. 3, Op 28
—1st movement, 457
Piano Sonata No. 8, Op 84
—1st movement, 451

Purcell
Dido and Aeneas: Overture, 319

Rameau
Castor et Pollux: Choeur des
Spartiates (Act I), 449

Ravel
Jeux d'eau, 415
Rigaudon (Tombeau de
Couperin), 290
Sonatina—1st movement, 498

Scarlatti, D.
Sonata, D minor, L. 413, 2
Sonata, G Major, L. 490, 487

Schubert
Fantasia-Sonata—1st move-
ment, 438
German Dance No. 7, 316
Impromptu, Op 90, No. 2, 330
Die Krähe (Winterreise), 448
Ländler, Op 18, No. 2, 223
Ländler, Op 18, No. 10, 282
Ländler, Op 67, No. 5, 144

Example number

Liebesbotschaft,	476
Moment Musical No. 2,	502
Pause (Die schöne Müllerin),	385
Piano Sonata, D Major, Op 63	
—2nd movement,	294
Piano Sonata, B♭ Major	
—1st movement,	337, 394
Piano Sonata, C minor	
—1st movement,	437
—2nd movement,	384
Symphony, B minor—1st	
movement,	497
Täuschung (Winterreise),	334
Tränenregen (Die schöne	
Müllerin),	366
Trio, B♭ Major, Op 99	
—1st movement,	389
Waltz, Op 9, No. 8,	6
Waltz, Op 10, No. 6,	295
Waltz, Op 18, No. 10,	V
Waltz, Op 50, No. 1,	141
Waltz, Op 77, No. 10,	333
Waltz, Op 127, No. 3,	293

Schumann

Album-Leaves, Op 124, No. 5,	307
Album-Leaves, Op 124, No. 10,	305
Album-Leaves, Op 124, No. 16,	9
Auf dem Rhein,	310
Bunte Blätter, Op 99,	279
Dichterliebe, No. 5,	287
Fantasiestücke, Op 12, No. 3,	299
Forest Scenes, No. 6	391
Humoreske, Op 20,	296
Kreisleriana, Op 16, No. 8,	252
Little Piece (Album for the	
Young),	5
Melody (Album for the	
Young),	234
Novelette, Op 21, No. 2,	358
Novelette, Op 21, No. 8,	363

Example number

Der Nussbaum,	286
Piano Concerto, A minor	
—1st movement,	325
Piano Quintet—1st movement,	439
Romance, Op 28, No. 1,	425
Scenes from Childhood, Op	
15, No. 1	303

Strauss, R.

Ariadne auf Naxos,	377
—Quintet,	406, 407
Don Juan,	381
Elektra	419

Stravinsky

Symphony in Three Movements—1st movement,	417, 472

Vaughan-Williams

Symphony No. 5,	331

Verdi

Oro supplex (Requiem),	429

Wagenaar

Ciacona,	413

Wagner

Götterdämmerung (Act I),	367
—Siegfried's Rhine Journey	360
Parsifal (Act I),	471
Tristan und Isolde: Prelude,	371
—Act II,	404

Weber

Der Freischütz: Overture,	335
—Act II, No. 6,	376

Wolf

In dem Schatten meiner	
Locken (Spanisches	
Liederbuch),	382
In der Frühe (Mörike	
Lieder),	488
Schlafendes Jesuskind	
(Mörike Lieder),	351

Notes and Glossary for the Voice-Leading Graphs

1. The note-values indicate the structural value and significance of tones and chords; they do not indicate rhythmic values.

2. The difference in structural significance is given in four different note-values: half-notes, quarter-notes, notes without stem and occasionally eighth-notes. The latter are used to indicate embellishments and appoggiaturas. The highest note-values in a graph represent tones or chords of the highest structural order. Among notes of equal value, those whose stems reach the same level are of the same structural order.

3. The relation between identical and different tones or chords, and specifically their structural connection, is indicated by dotted or solid slurs, lines, arrows or by beams.

4. Horizontal, solid arrows (used mostly in regard to bass motions) indicate the direction or driving tendency of the music in general, or passing motions in particular.

5. A note in parenthesis with or without a dotted stem means a note expected on the basis of direct voice leading, but omitted or substituted for in the composition.

6. Brackets of various kinds indicate either chord prolongations (‿) or melodic parallelisms (⌐——⌐).

7. Roman numerals are assigned to harmonic chords only; the relative size of these numerals corresponds to their structural value.

8. A small Roman numeral in parenthesis indicates the chord of harmonic emphasis.

Glossary of Symbols

P	Passing tone or passing chord
N	Neighbor note or neighbor-note chord
UN and LN	Upper and lower neighbor note
IN	Incomplete neighbor note
$\frac{N}{P}$	Neighbor-passing chord
Em	Embellishing chord
CS	Contrapuntal-structural chord
DF	Double function chord
M	Mixture
‖	Interruption
D	Dividing dominant
A B or A B A[1]	Indication of form

List of Sources (*Abbreviations*)

AM	*Altniederländische Motetten,* ed. by W. Braunfels. Oratoriumsverlag, Köln.
AMI	*L'Arte musicale in Italia,* ed. by L. Torchi. G. Ricordi e C., Milano.
AUDM	*Aufführungspraxis der Musik,* by R. Haas. Akademische Verlagsgesellschaft Athenaion, Potsdam.
CM	*Cent Motets du XIIIe Siècle,* transcribed by P. Aubry. Rouart, Lerolle & Cie., Paris.
DAS CHORWERK	*Das Chorwerk,* ed. by F. Blume. G. Kallmeyer Verlag, Wolfenbüttel.
DTOE	*Denkmäler der Tonkunst in Oesterreich.* Artaria & Co., Wien.
HAM	*Historical Anthology of Music; Oriental, Medieval and Renaissance Music,* ed. by A. T. Davison and W. Apel, Vol. I. Rev. ed. Harvard University Press, Cambridge, Mass.
HDM	*Handbuch der Musikgeschichte,* ed. by G. Adler, 2nd ed. Heinrich Keller, Berlin.
EPM	*The Evolution of Piano Music (1350–1700),* ed. by C. Sachs. E. B. Marks Music Corp., N. Y.
MET	*Music of Earlier Times (13th Century to Bach),* ed. by J. Wolf. Broude Bros., N. Y.
MMA	*Music in the Middle Ages,* by G. Reese. W. W. Norton & Co., N. Y.
MW	Guillaume de Machaut, *Musikalische Werke,* ed. by F. Ludwig. Breitkopf & Härtel, Leipzig.
OHM	*The Oxford History of Music.* Oxford University Press, Ltd., London.
OL	Orlando di Lasso, *Sämmtliche Werke.* Breitkopf & Härtel, Leipzig.
SHM	*A Short History of Music,* by A. Einstein. 2nd ed. Alfred A. Knopf, N. Y.

TC   *Sechs Trienter Codices*, ed. by G. Adler. In DTOE.

VDO   *Studien zur Vorgeschichte der Orchestersuite im 15. und
          16. Jahrhundert*, by F. Blume. Kistner & Siegel, Leipzig.

WJO   Jacob Obrecht, *Werken*, ed. by J. Wolf. Johannes Müller,
          Amsterdam.

WJP   Josquin des Prés, *Werken*, ed. by A. Smijers. G. Alsbach &
          Co., Amsterdam.

Note: Sources for the quotations from English virginal compositions, which
have been repeatedly reprinted, are omitted.

Musical Illustrations

I   BACH Prelude No. 21 (Well-Tempered Clavier, Bk I)

II   BACH Chorale (No. 294)

BACH Chorale (No. 23)

applied Dominant

passing chord

I → II⁶₅ V I

b

N P

I → II⁶₅ V I

c

I II⁶₅ V I

IV

e

graph III a

f

chorale

SCHUBERT Waltz, Op 18, No. 10

VII

I V I · I V I

I

VIII MOZART Piano Sonata, A minor, K. 331 310

5

IX

X HINDEMITH Piano Sonata No. 3

With quiet motion

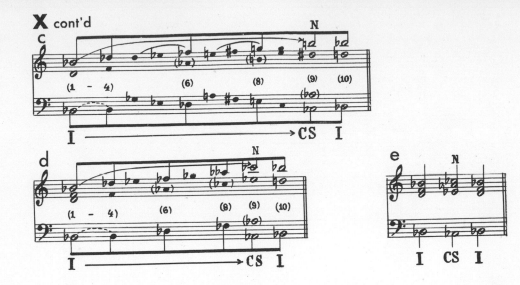

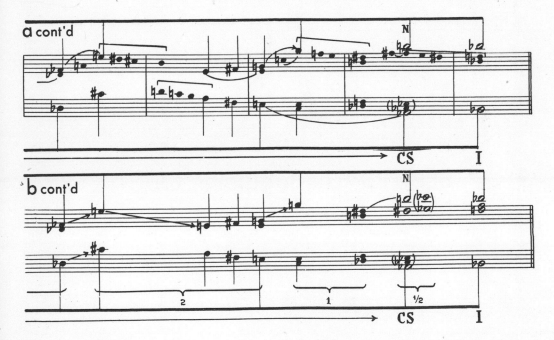

1 # BACH Chorale (No. 6)

I ⟶ V I

2 # D. SCARLATTI Sonata, D minor, L. 413

becomes

I ⟶ V

3 # BEETHOVEN Bagatelle, Op 119, No. 11

Andante, ma non troppo

4

5 ## SCHUMANN Little Piece (Album for the Young)

6 ## SCHUBERT Waltz, Op 9, No. 8

7　HAYDN Minuet

bars 5-6

8　FOLK TUNE

9　SCHUMANN Album-Leaves,
Op 124　No. 16

Allegretto

10　BEETHOVEN Piano Sonata,
A Major, Op 2, No. 2

Largo appassionato

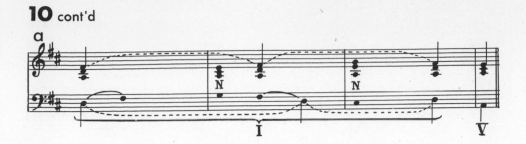

a

11   BACH Chorale (No. 7)

a

horizontalization of

b

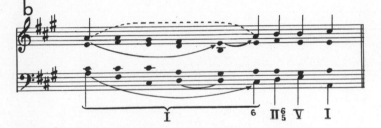

c

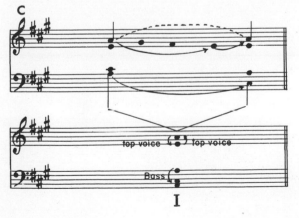

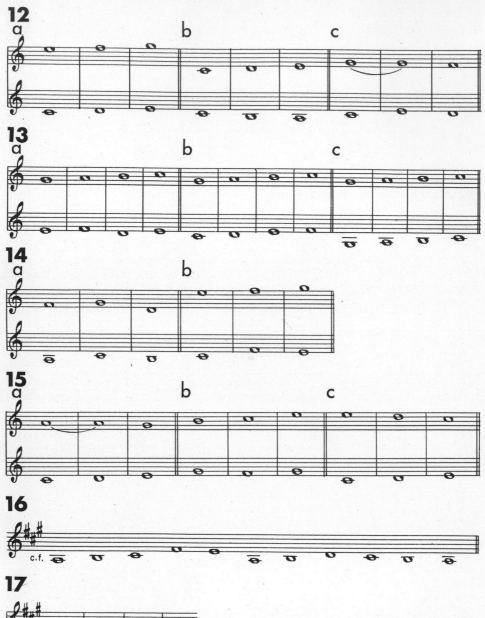

18

19

20

21

22

23

24

a
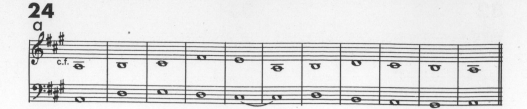

b
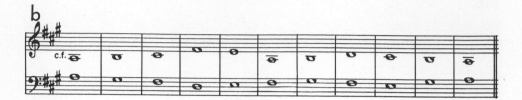

25

a   b

26

a   b

27

a   b

28

29

30

31

32 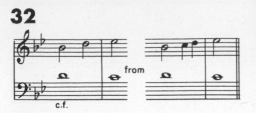 **33**

34

35

36  **37**

38

39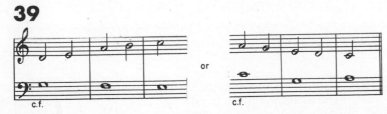

40

41

42

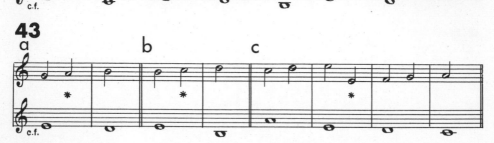

43

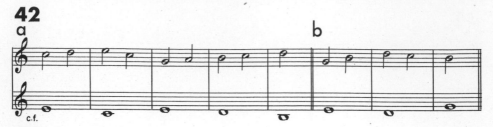

avoids

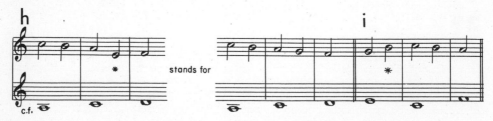

stands for

44

45

46
a   b   c   d

N   N   N   N

c.f.

47
a   b

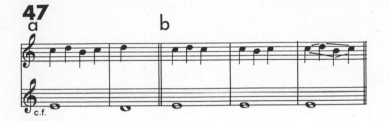

c.f.

48
a   b

c.f.

49
a   progression   b embellishment

c.f.

50

c.f.

51

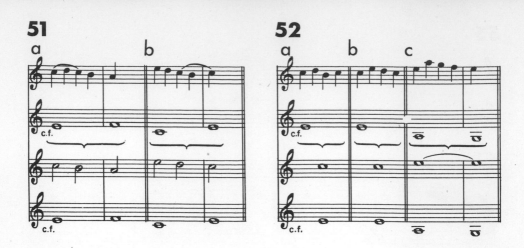

52

53 **54**

55

56

57

a

b

58

59

60

61

62

63

64

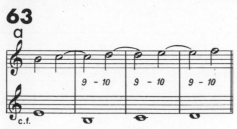

65

65 cont'd

66

a good   b   c   d

a not good   b   c   d

67

a   b   c   d

e   f   g   h

68   **69**

a   b   c

70

a   b   c

71   **72**

73

74

75

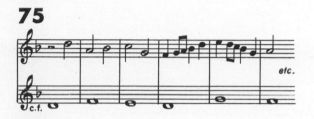

76

77

78

79

80

81

82

83

84

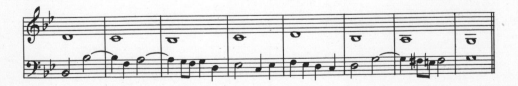

85

86

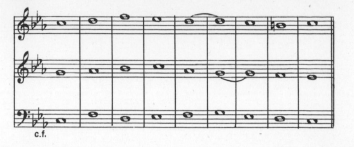

c.f.

87

c.f.

88

c.f.

89

c.f.

90

91

92

93

26

Part II Chapter Four

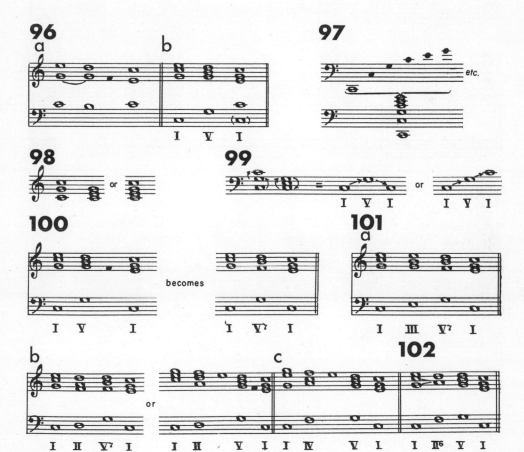

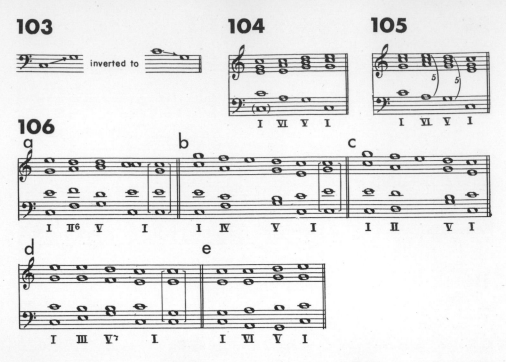

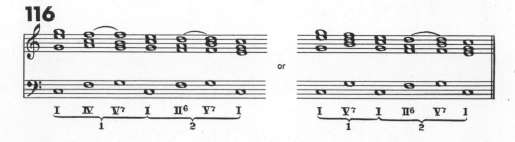

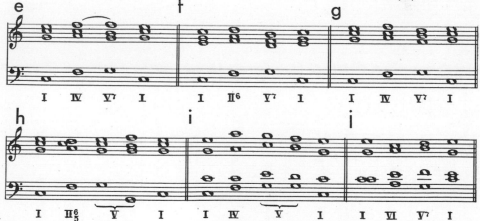

118

a
I ——→ II⁶ V⁷   I

b
I ——→ II⁶ V⁷   I

c
I ——————→ II⁶ V   I

119   BACH Chorale (No. 337)

I ——→ II⁶₅ V⁷ I

120   BACH Chorale (No. 88)

I ——→ II⁶₅ V   I   from   I ——→ II⁶₅ V⁷   I

121

I ——→ II V⁷ I   I ——→ II V⁷ I

or

122 BACH Chorale (No. 348)

I ——→ II V I

123 BACH Chorale (No. 246)

I ——————→ II⁶ V I

a

I   II⁶₅ V I

124

I ————————————→ V⁷ I

125

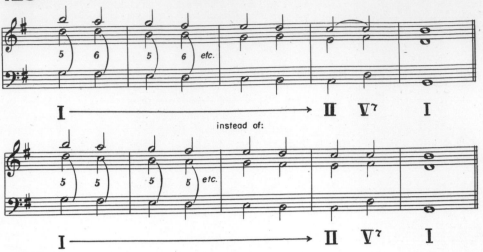

I ⟶ II V⁷ I

instead of:

I ⟶ II V⁷ I

126

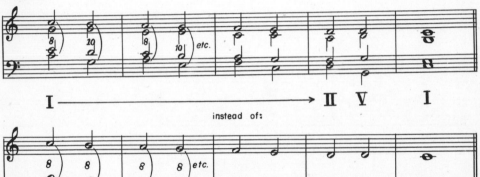

I ⟶ II V I

instead of:

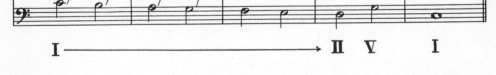

I ⟶ II V I

127

I ⟶ II⁷ V I

I ————————————————→ III⁶₃ V   I
                          or
                          II⁶

128

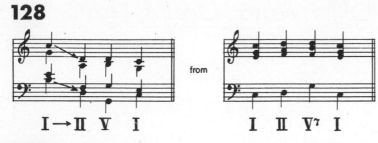

from

I → II V I   I II V⁷ I

129

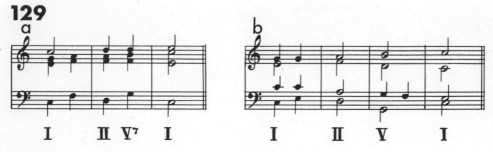

a   b

I   II V⁷ I   I   II   V   I

c

5 6   5 6   5 6

I ————————————————→ V   I
                     ⁶₄ ⁷

d

⁶₅   ⁶₅   ⁶₅

I ————————————————→ V   I
                     ⁶₄ ⁷

45345

130

131 # CHOPIN Waltz, Op 34, No. 2

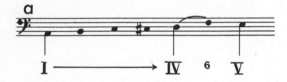

132 # BACH Gavotte (French Suite No. 5)

133   BRAHMS Piano Sonata, F minor, Op 5

Allegro maestoso

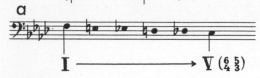

a

I ⟶ V (⁶₄ ⁵₃)

134

I * II V I

135

136

136 cont'd

137

138

139

140 BACH Chorale (No. 330)

141 SCHUBERT Waltz, Op 50, No. 1

142 CHOPIN Waltz, E Major (Posth.)

143 MOZART Piano Sonata, C Major, K. 545

144 SCHUBERT Ländler Op 67 No. 5

145 BACH Chorale (No. 346)

146

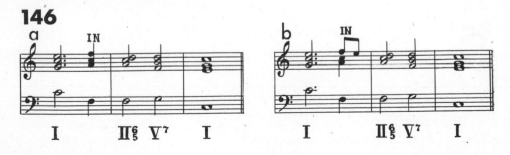

147 BACH Little Prelude, C minor

148

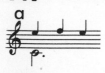

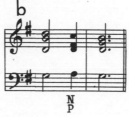

149

150

151

152 BACH Prelude No. 1 (Well-Tempered Clavier, Bk I)

153

154 C. P. E. BACH Minuetto

155 CHOPIN Waltz, Op 69, No. 2

Moderato

156 JOSQUIN Missa: Pange lingua

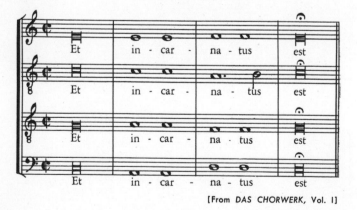

Et in - car - na - tus est

Et in - car - na - tus est

Et in - car - na - tus est

Et in - car - na - tus est

[From DAS CHORWERK, Vol. I]

157

158 BACH Prelude No. 6 (Well-Tempered Clavier, Bk I)

a

159

a   b

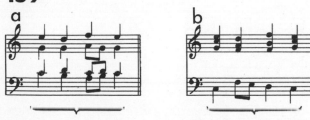

160 BACH Chorale (No. 11)

160 cont'd

161

162 BACH Chorale (No. 366)

163 BACH Chorale (No. 367)

164

a  b

I II V⁷ I
(II⁶)

165

a  b

I IV V I

166

 becomes   becomes

167

a b c

d or e f

 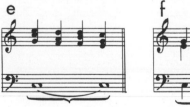 

g h

168 ## BACH Chorale (No. 24)

169 ## BACH Prelude No. 2 (Well-Tempered Clavier, Bk II)

170 ## BACH Little Prelude, F Major

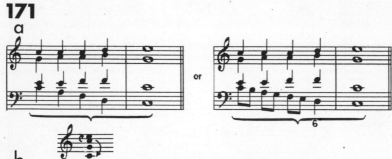

171

171 cont'd

172

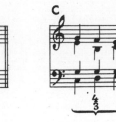

or

173

174 BACH Chorale (No. 233)

175 BACH Chorale (No. 367)

176 BACH Chorale (No. 362)

46

177 BACH Chorale (Peters No. 118)

a

I   IV⁷ V I

b

I   IV⁷ V I

178

a

I   II⁶

b

I   II

c

I   II⁶

179   BACH Chorale (No. 110)

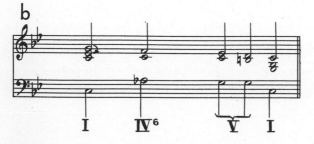

180

181

b

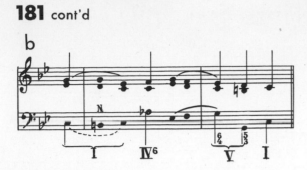

182 BACH Chorale (No. 42)

a

b

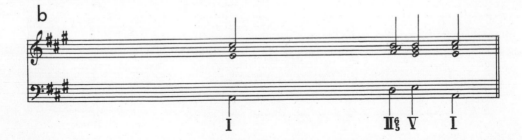

183 MOZART Piano Sonata, D Major, K. 311.

184 JOSQUIN Motet: Tu pauperum refugium

Tu pau-pe-rum re-fu-gi-um,

[From HAM, Vol. I, No. 90]

185 GIACOMO FOGLIANO Ave Maria

San-cta Ma-ri-a, Ma-ter De-i, o-ra pro no-bis

[From *HAM*, Vol. I, No. 94]

186 BARTÓK Piano Pieces for Children, No. 32

Allegro ironico

186 cont'd

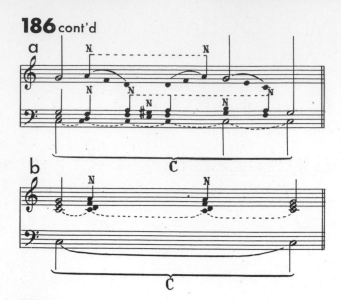

187

188

189

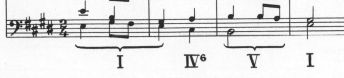

a

b

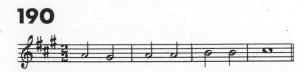

190

a

b

191

a

$$I \qquad II_5^6 \quad V \qquad I$$

b
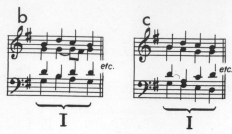
etc.
$$I$$

c

etc.
$$I$$

d

$$I \qquad II_5^6 \ V \qquad I$$

e
etc
$$I$$

192

a
$$I \qquad IV \qquad V \qquad I$$

b

$$I \qquad II^7 \quad V \qquad I$$

193

a

$$\text{I} \qquad \text{II}_5^6 \quad \text{V} \qquad \text{I}$$

b

$$\text{I} \qquad \text{II}^6 \quad \text{V} \qquad \text{I}$$

194

a

$$\text{I} \qquad \text{II}_5^6 \qquad \underset{\substack{5\\4}\ \substack{5\\3}}{\text{V}} \qquad \text{I}$$

b

etc.

$$\underset{6}{\text{I}}$$

c

etc.

$$\underset{\substack{5\\3}}{\text{I}}$$

194 cont'd

d

$$I \longrightarrow II^6_5 \quad V \quad I \qquad \text{from} \qquad I \rightarrow II^6_5 V I$$

195

a

b

c

196

a Interval-filling   b Interval-outlining   c ornamental

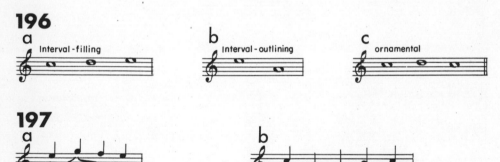

197

a   b

198   MOZART Piano Sonata, F Major, K. 280

199 MOZART Piano Sonata, C Major, K. 279

200 BACH Courante (Partita No. 5)

201 MOZART Piano Sonata, C Major, K. 279

202 **HANDEL Double**

203 **MOZART Rondo, A minor, K. 511**

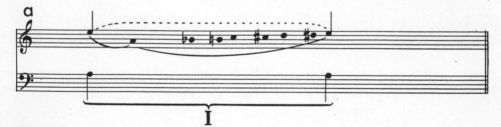

204

205 MENDELSSOHN Song Without Words, Op 62, No. 1

206 BEETHOVEN Piano Sonata, F minor, Op 2, No. 1

207 MOZART Fantasia, D minor, K. 397

208 MOZART Piano Sonata, C minor, K. 457

209 CARISSIMI Cantata: Mary Stuart

Ah mo - ri - re, ah mo - ri - re, ah mo - ri - - - - re

[From OHM, Vol. III]

210 HAYDN Piano Sonata, C Major, No. 35

Allegro con brio

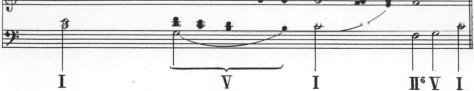

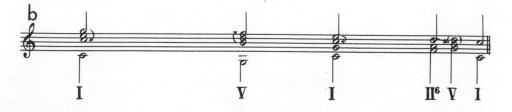

210 cont'd

c

instead of

II^6 V I II^6 V I

211   HAYDN Piano Sonata, D Major, No. 19

Andante

p

a

I II^6 V I

b   c

becomes

I II^6 V I

212   FROBERGER Suite: "Auf die Mayerin"

[From *DTOe*, Vol. VI]

a   N

I II^6 V I

213 MOZART Courante (Suite, K. 399)

I   II V   I III⁶ → V I   I II⁶→V I

214 HAYDN Piano Sonata, G Major, No. 27

I   II⁶   V   I

215 FOLK TUNE

I   II⁶   V   I

216 CHOPIN Nocturne, Op 32, No. 1

217 MOZART Piano Sonata, F Major, K. 280

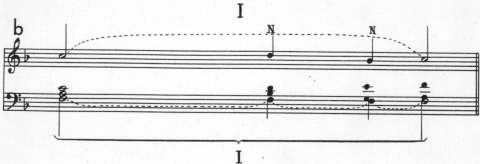

218 # MENDELSSOHN Song Without Words, Op 102, No. 2

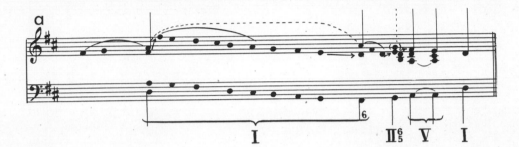

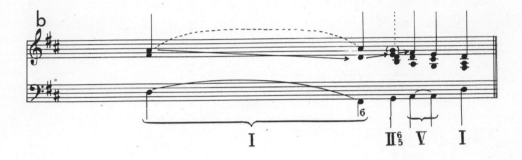

219 # MOZART Aria ("Don Giovanni")

Dal - la sua pa - ce la mia di - pen - de;

quel -che a lei   pia - ce,___   vi - ta mi ren - de, etc.

220 CLEMENTI Sonatina, G Major, Op 36, No. 2

221 BEETHOVEN Piano Sonata,
E Major, Op 109

222 BEETHOVEN Symphony No. 9

223 **SCHUBERT** Ländler, Op 18, No. 2

I V I

224 **C. P. E. BACH** Fantasia

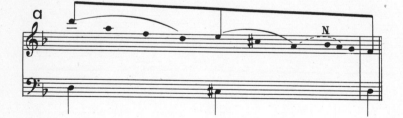

225 BACH Praeludium (Partita No. 1)

a

226 BEETHOVEN Piano Sonata,
G Major, Op 79

Presto alla tedesca

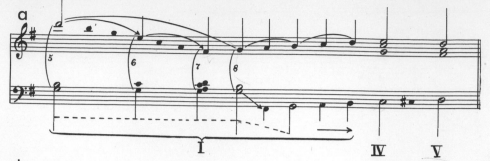

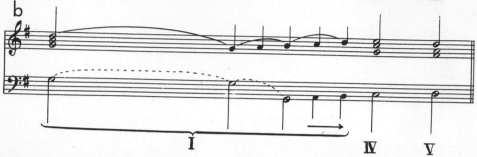

227 HANDEL Variation 1 (Air from Suite No. 3)

a

b

228 BACH Courante (Suite pour le clavecin, E♭ Major)

229 BEETHOVEN Piano Sonata, E Major, Op 14, No. 1

229 cont'd

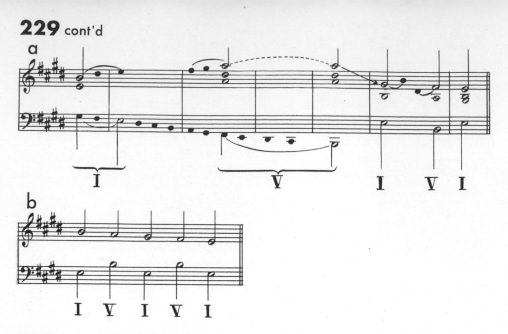

a

I   V   I   V   I

b

I   V   I   V   I

230   MOZART Trio, E♭ Major, K. 498

Andante

p

a   b   c

231   BACH Praeambulum (Partita No. 5)

a

♮4 9 7 °5
C⁶   C⁶

232 ## BACH Aria variata

233 ## MOZART Piano Sonata, C Major, K 545

234 ## SCHUMANN Melody (Album for the Young)

235 MOZART Fugue, C Major
(Fantasia, K. 394)

which avoids

236 BACH Chorale (No. 64)

10 8 6

237 BACH Chorale (Peters No. 43)

238 **HANDEL Minuet**

a   b

I   IV   V   I   IV   V

239 **COPLAND Appalachian Spring**

Fl.

Strgs.

[P. 81, SCORE]

a   b

10   8   7   5   8

I⁶   IV   V   I

240 **BACH Brandenburg Concerto No. 1.**

Adagio

a

241 # BARTÓK Ukrainian Song (Petite Suite)

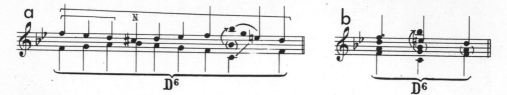

242

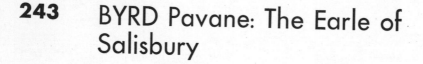

243 # BYRD Pavane: The Earle of Salisbury

244 MOZART Piano Sonata, G Major, K. 283

245 GOTTLIEB MUFFAT Air (Suite, B♭ Major)

246 BACH Prelude No. 10 (Well-Tempered Clavier, Bk I)

246 cont'd

a

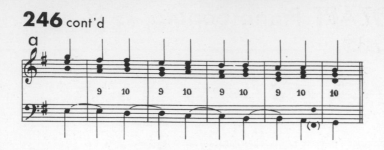

247 HAYDN Piano Sonata, C Major, No. 21

a

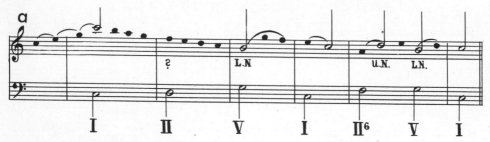

b

c

248 MOZART Piano Sonata, G Major, K. 283

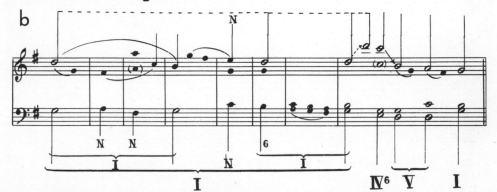

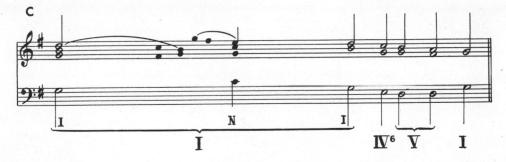

249 BACH Little Prelude, C minor

250 CHOPIN Mazurka, Op 41, No. 4

251 CHOPIN Etude, Op 25, No. 5

252 SCHUMANN Kreisleriana, Op 16, No. 8

Schnell und spielend

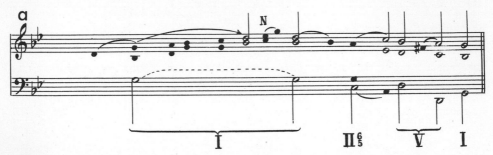

253

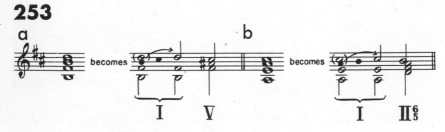

254 BEETHOVEN Piano Sonata, G Major, Op 14, No. 2

Allegro

a

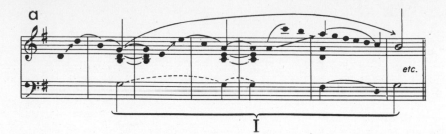

etc.

I

b

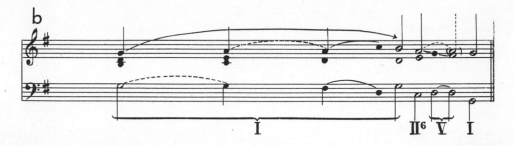

I   II⁶ V I

c

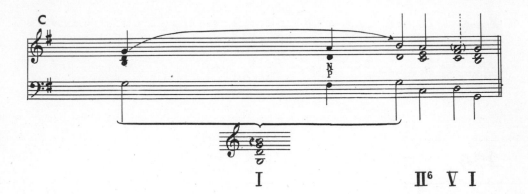

N
P

I   II⁶ V I

d (4) (6)

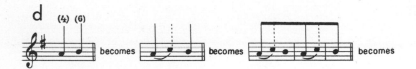

becomes   becomes   becomes

255

256

257

258

259

I II⁶ V I

260

I V I II⁶ V I

261

262

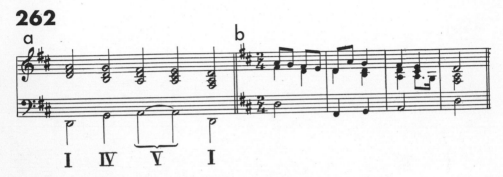

263

264

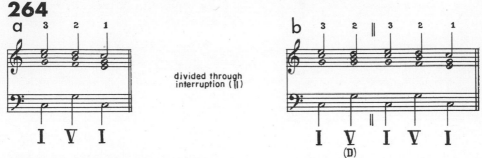

divided through
interruption (‖)

I IV I

I V I V I
(D)

265 BEETHOVEN Piano Sonata,
E Major, Op 14, No. 1

Allegretto

a

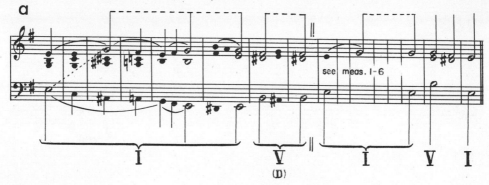

see meas. 1-6

I V I V I
(D)

266 **HAYDN Symphony, G Major, No. 100**

267 **MOZART Quartet ("Don Giovanni")**

Non ___ ti fi - dar, o mi - se - ra, di quel ri - bal - do cor!

Me già tra - dì quel bar - ba - ro, te vuol tra - dir an - cor!

268 BASSE DANSE

[From *VDO*, App. P. 35]

269 ## BACH Chorale (No. 192)

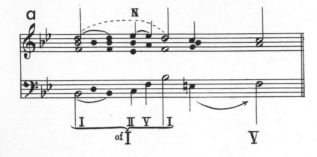

270

271 ## GIBBONS The Queene's Command

272 HAYDN Piano Sonata, E♭ Major, No. 52

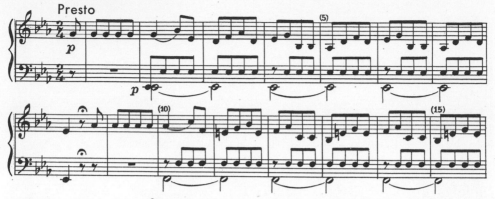

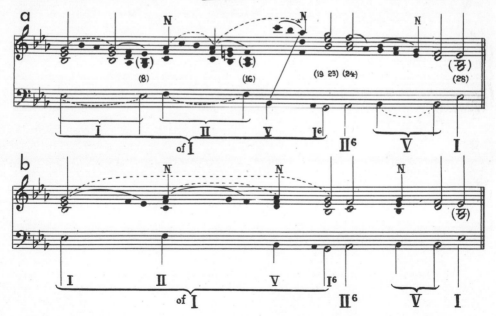

JOSQUIN Motet: Ave Maria

Ma - ri - a ple - na gra - ti - a, coe - le - sti - a, ter -

Ma - ri - a ple - na gra - ti - a, coe - le - sti - a, ter -

Ma - ri - a ple - na gra - ti - a, coe - le - sti - a, ter - re -

Ma - ri - a ple - na gra - ti - a, coe - le - sti - a, ter -

re - stri - a, mun - dum re - plens lae - ti - ti - a.

re - stri - a, mun - dum re - plens lae - ti - ti - a.

- stri - a, mun - dum re - plens lae - ti - ti - a.

re - stri - a, mun - dum re - plens lae - ti - ti - a.

[From AM, P. 9]

a

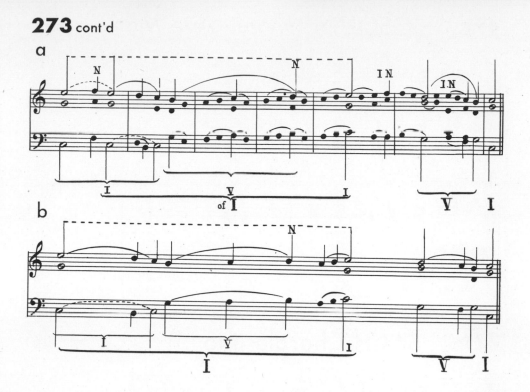

b

274 CLÉREAU Missa: In me transierunt

Ky - ri - e - e - ley - - - - - son, e - ley - - - - - - - - son

[From *HDM*, Vol. I, P. 330]

a

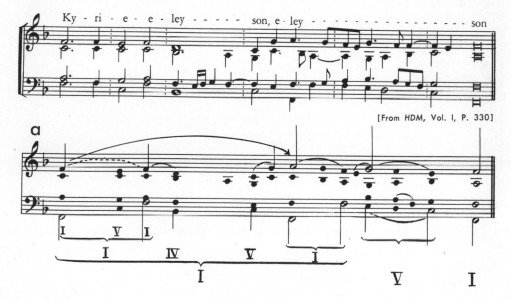

275

276   BACH Chorale (No. 5)

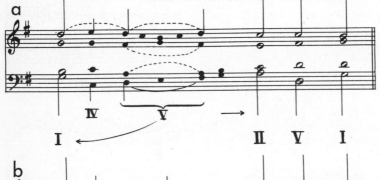

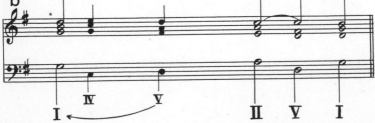

277 MOZART Piano Sonata, D Major, K. 576

278

279 SCHUMANN Bunte Blätter, Op 99

280 **BACH Prelude No. 7 (Well-Tempered Clavier, Bk II)**

a

I   V   II   V   I

281

a   b

I   V   IV   V   I   I   V   II   V   I

282 **SCHUBERT Ländler, Op 18, No. 10**

V   I

283 **CHOPIN Etude, Op 10, No. 4**

Presto

f

V   I

284 CHOPIN Mazurka, Op 63, No. 2

285 CHOPIN Mazurka, Op 24, No. 3

286 SCHUMANN Der Nussbaum

287 SCHUMANN Dichterliebe, No. 5

Ich will mei - ne See - - - le tau - - - chen

a

II^r V

I

b

I V I

288 BEETHOVEN Piano Sonata,
Eᵇ Major, Op 31, No. 3

Allegro

ritard.

cresc.

sf

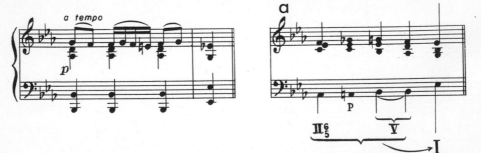

a tempo

a

II^6_5 V

I

289 BEETHOVEN Piano Sonata, E♭ Major, Op 81a

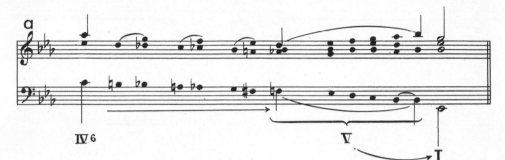

IV⁶ V I

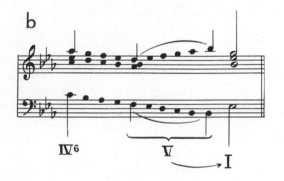

b
IV⁶ V I

c
IV⁶ V I

290 RAVEL Rigaudon (Tombeau de Couperin)

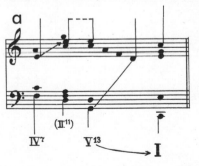

a
IV⁷ (II¹¹) V¹³ I

291

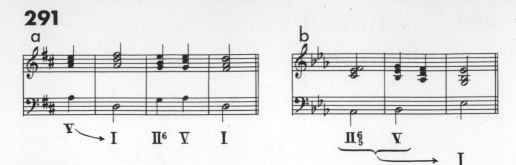

292

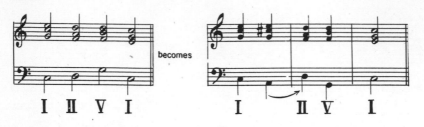

becomes

I   II   V   I   I   II   V   I

293   SCHUBERT Waltz Op 127, No. 3

a

I   II   V   I

294 SCHUBERT Piano Sonata,
D Major,

295 SCHUBERT Waltz, Op 10, No. 6

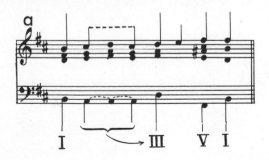

296 SCHUMANN Humoreske, Op 20

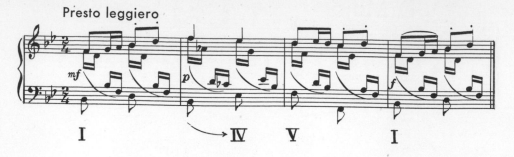

297 CHOPIN Waltz, Op 64, No. 2

298 BEETHOVEN Piano Sonata,
C Major, Op 2, No. 3

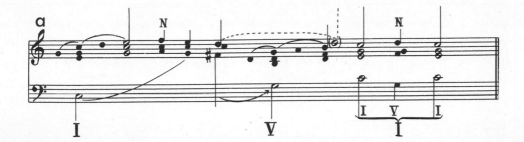

299 SCHUMANN Fantasiestücke,
Op 12, No. 3

300 LISZT Liebestraum (Nocturne No. 3)

Poco allegro, con affetto

I   V I

301

I   II V   I   I   VI V   I

I   III V   I   I   IV   V   I

302

contrapunctal   harmonic

303   SCHUMANN Scenes from
Childhood, Op 15, No. 1

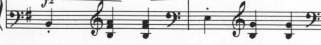

304   CHOPIN Mazurka, Op 17, No. 2

Lento, ma non troppo

305 SCHUMANN Album-Leaves,
Op 124, No. 10

306

SCHUMANN Album-Leaves, Op 124, No. 5

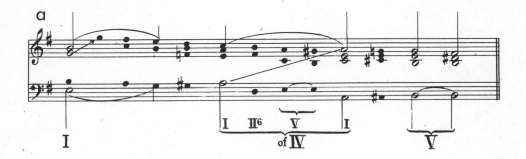

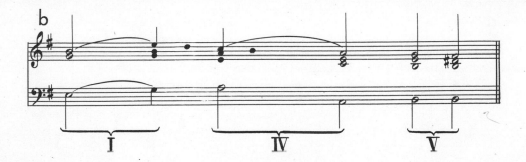

308 # BRAHMS Intermezzo, Op 118, No. 2

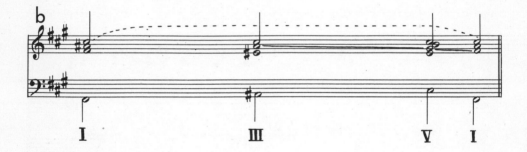

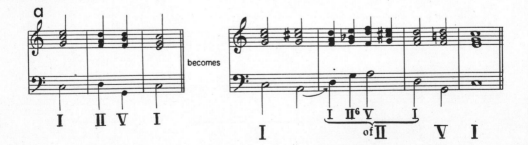

309

I   IV   V   I   I   I   II⁶   V   I   V   I
                                    of IV

310 SCHUMANN Auf dem Rhein

Ziemlich langsam

Auf dei - nem Grun-de ha - ben sie an - ver - borg' - nem __ Ort

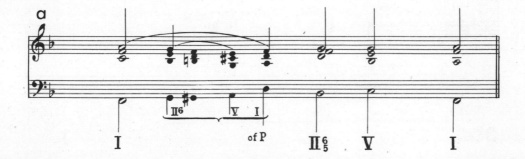

I   II⁶   V   I   II⁶₅   V   I
         of P

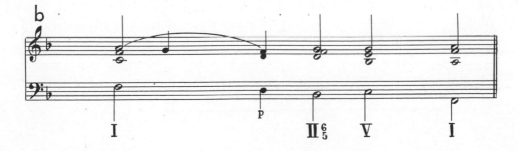

I   P   II⁶₅   V   I

311 CHOPIN Mazurka, Op 59, No. 2

312 BACH Chorale (No. 55)

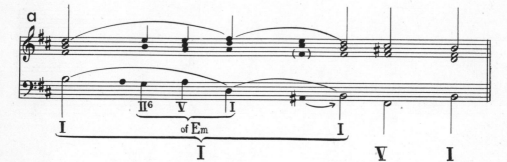

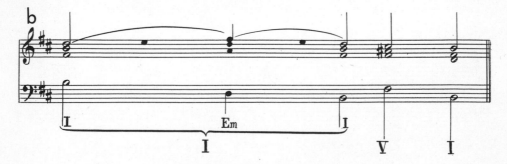

313   BACH Chorale (No. 177)

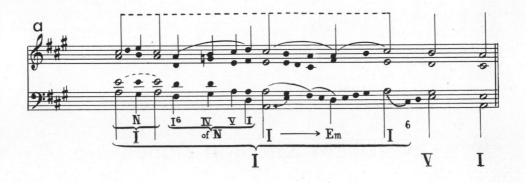

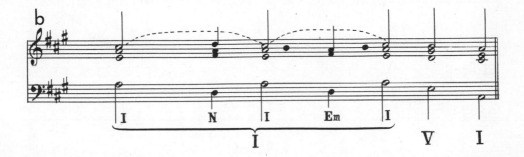

314

315 CHOPIN Mazurka, Op 68, No. 2 (Posth.)

316 SCHUBERT German Dance, No. 7

316 cont'd

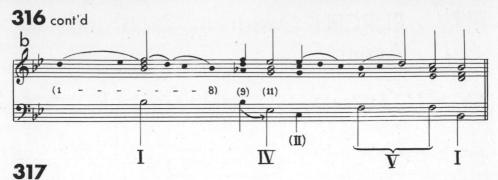

b

(1 - - - - - - 8) (9) (11)

I   IV   (II)   V   I

317

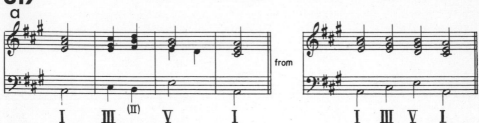

a

from

I III (II) V I   I III V I

b

from

I IV (II) V I   I IV V I

318 HAYDN Piano Sonata, G minor, No. 44

Allegretto

a

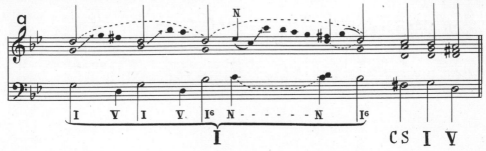

N

I V I V I⁶ N - - - - - - N I⁶

I   CS I V

113

319   PURCELL Overture, "Dido and Aeneas"

a

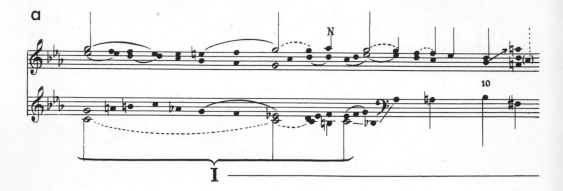

b

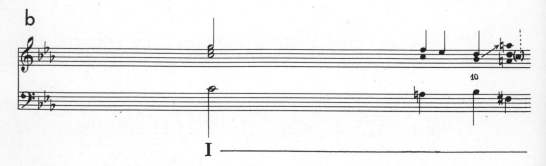

320   PEERSON The Primerose

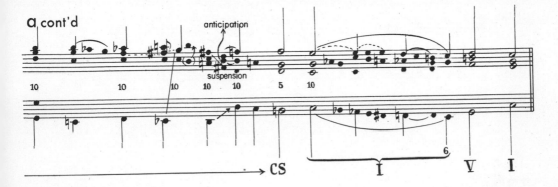

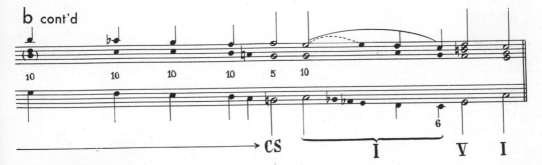

320 cont'd

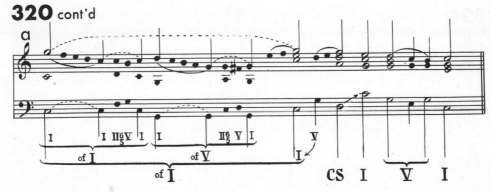

321 BACH Chorale (No. 229)

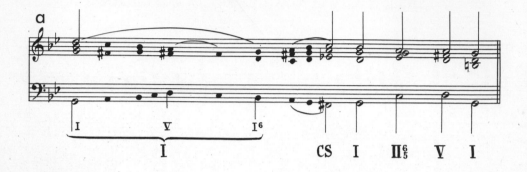

I   V   I⁶

I

CS   I   II⁶₅   V   I

322

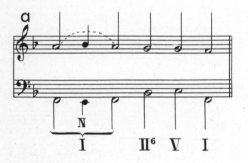

a

N

I   II⁶   V   I

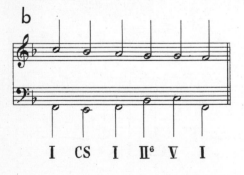

b

I   CS   I   II⁶   V   I

323 COUPERIN La Bandoline

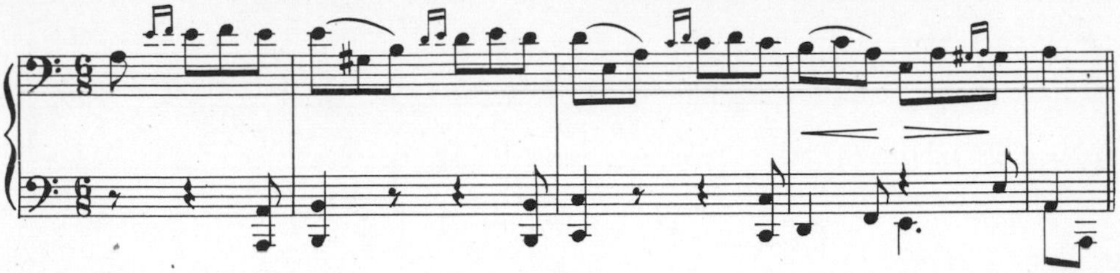

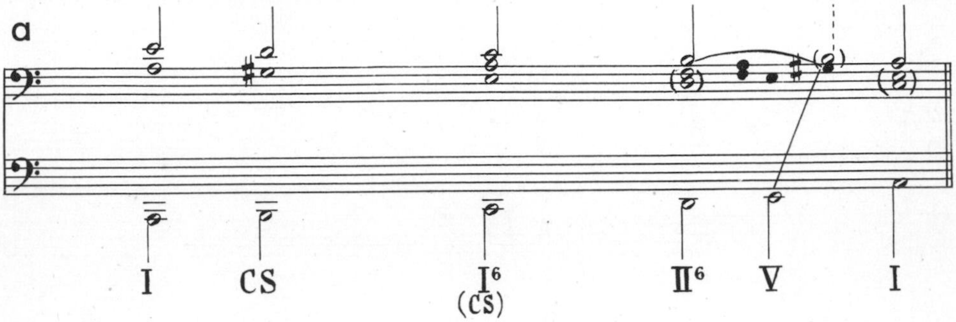
a
I
CS
I6
(CS)
II6
V
I

324 CHOPIN Nocturne, Op 9, No. 2

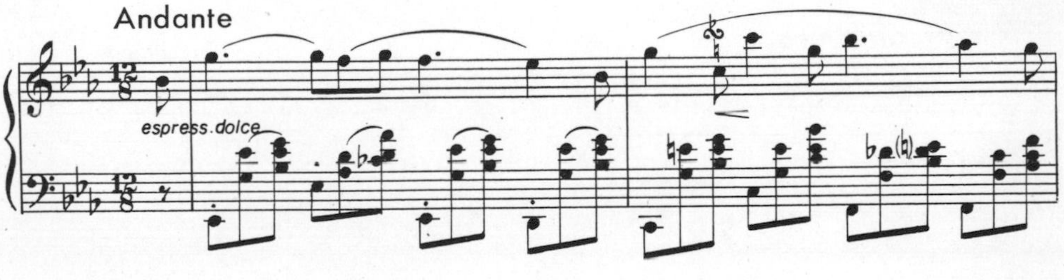
Andante
espress.dolce

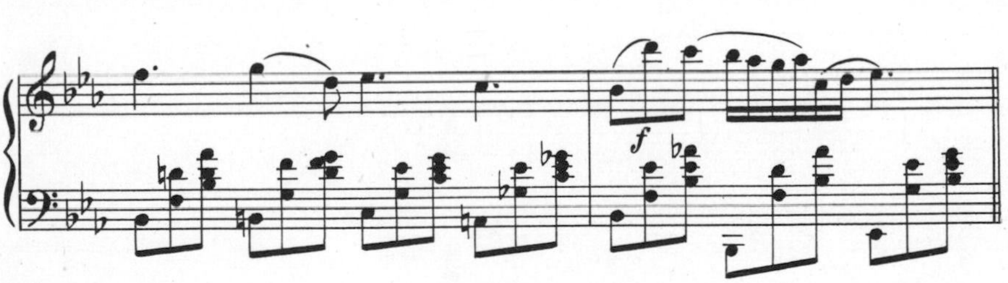
f

a

b

325 SCHUMANN Piano Concerto

Allegro affetuoso

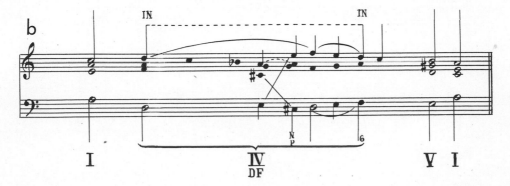

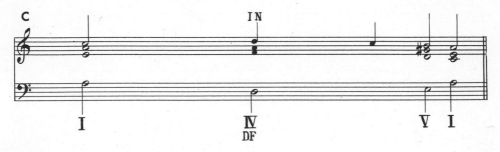

326

327   BACH Chorale (No. 320)

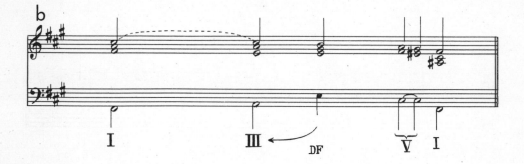

328   BACH Chorale (No. 280)

a

b

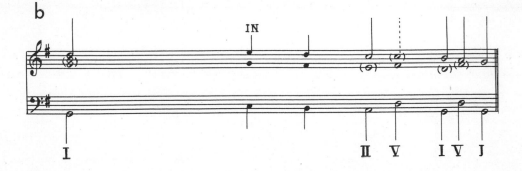

330 SCHUBERT Impromptu, Op 90, No. 2

331   **VAUGHAN-WILLIAMS**
Symphony No. 5

[P. 8, SCORE]

332   **MOZART Rondo, K. 494**

332 cont'd

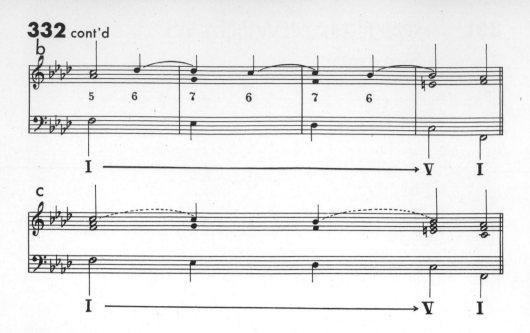

333 SCHUBERT Waltz Op 77, No. 10

334   ## SCHUBERT Täuschung

I ⟶ VI V I

335   ## WEBER Overture, "Der Freischütz"

336 ## HAYDN String Quartet, Op 76, No. 4

337 ## SCHUBERT Piano Sonata, B♭ Major

338

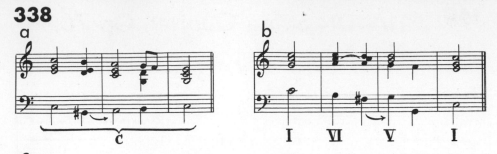

339 BACH Chorale (No. 361)

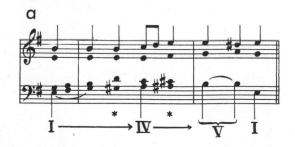

340

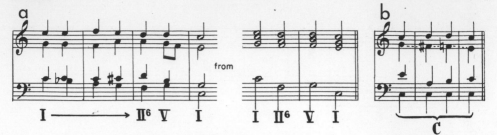

341

342

343

344

or
(meas. 2)

345

346

347 BACH Chorale (No. 166)

I   II⁶₅ ——————→ V   I

348 BACH Chorale (No. 167)

I ——————————→ IV ——————→ V I

349 HAYDN String Quartet, Op 76, No. 1

Adagio sostenuto

a

N ——→ N

I   V

b

N   N

I   V

CHOPIN Mazurka, Op 24, No. 3

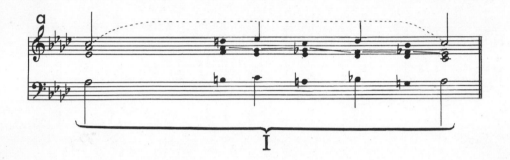

WOLF Schlafendes Jesuskind

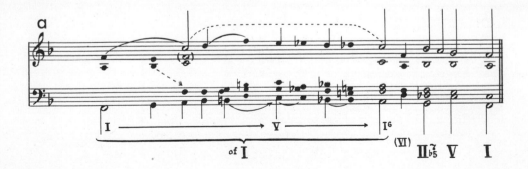

352

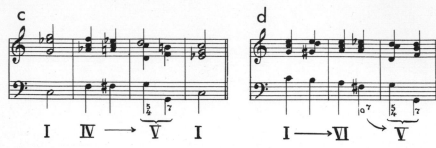

353

354

355

 from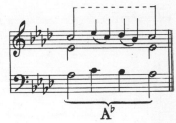

356

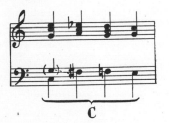

CHOPIN Mazurka, Op 30, No. 4

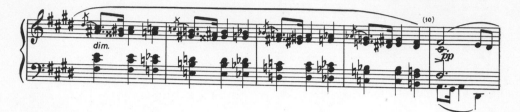

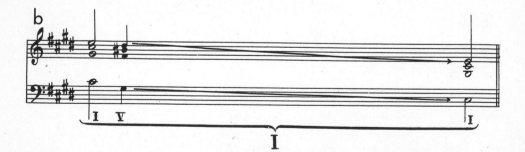

358 ## SCHUMANN Novelette, Op 21, No. 2

Ausserst rasch und mit Bravour

a

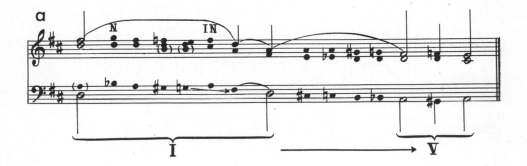

b

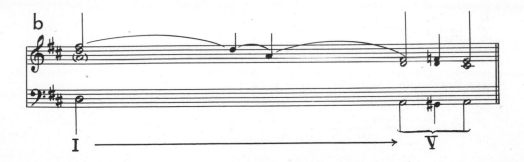

359 **CHOPIN** Mazurka, Op 17, No. 4

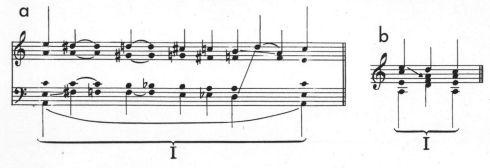

360 **WAGNER** Siegfried's Rhine
Journey ("Götterdämmerung")

CHOPIN Mazurka, Op 7, No. 2

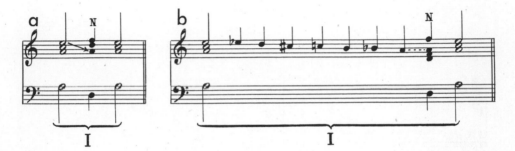

362 CHOPIN Mazurka, Op 6, No. 1

d

e

363 SCHUMANN Novelette, Op 21, No. 8

Munter, nicht zu rasch

a

I   V

b

I   V

c

I   V

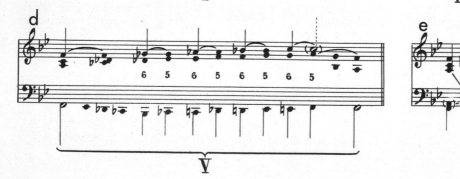

d   e

V

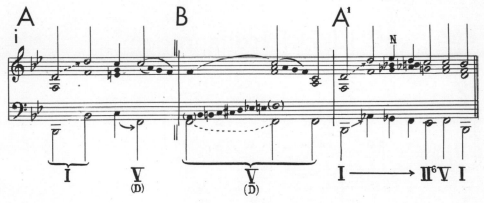

364

a

I   V   I

b

I ———————→ V   I

c

I ———————→ V   I

365

 becomes

366   SCHUBERT Tränenregen

Ziemlich langsam

I   II   V

367   WAGNER "Götterdämmerung,"
            (Act I)

368

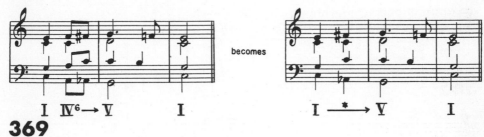

becomes

369

370

371 WAGNER Prelude, "Tristan und Isolde"

372

373

374

instead of

375 BEETHOVEN Piano Sonata,
C# minor, Op 27, No. 2

Adagio sostenuto

pp

a

N

I → II⁶ₚₕᵣ. V I

376 WEBER "Der Freischütz" (Act II,
No. 6)

Allegretto

o — wie an - ders fühlt — mein Herz — o —

— wie an - - ders — fühlt mein — Herz

a

N N

mf

I II⁶ₚₕᵣ. V I

R. STRAUSS "Ariadne auf Naxos"

Mezzo movimento

[P. 216, PIANO-VOCAL SCORE]

a

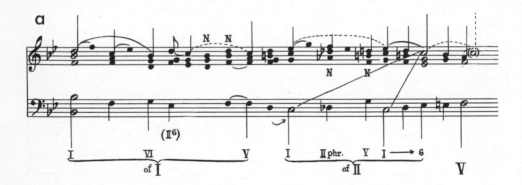

b

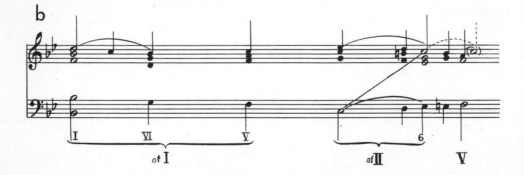

CHOPIN Nocturne, Op 27, No. 1

380 PROKOFIEFF Gavotte, Op 77, No. 4

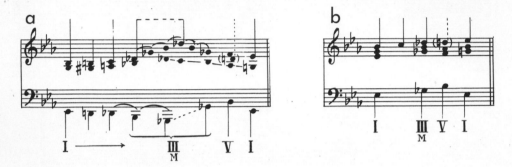

381 R. STRAUSS Don Juan

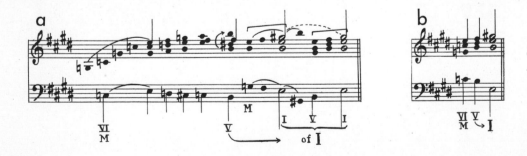

WOLF In dem Schatten meiner Locken

Leicht, zart, nicht schnell

In dem Schat - ten mei - ner Lo - cken schlief mir mein Ge - lieb - ter

ein. Weck' ich ihn nun auf?

Ach nein!

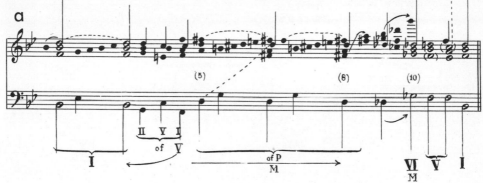

383 BEETHOVEN Piano Sonata, C minor, Op 13

Adagio cantabile

384 SCHUBERT Piano Sonata,
C minor

a

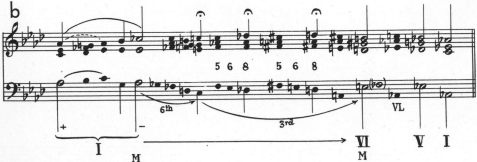

b

c

385 SCHUBERT Pause

Ziemlich geschwind

Nun lie-be Lau-te, ruh' an dem Na-gel- hier, und weht ein

Lüft - chen ü - ber die Sai - ten _ dir, und streift ei - ne Bie - ne mit

ih - ren Flü - geln dich, da wird mir so ban - ge, und es durchschau-ert mich.

War - um liess ich das Band auch hän - gen so lang? Oft

fliegt's um die Sai - ten mit seuf - zen-dem Klang. Ist es der Nach - klang _

387 CHOPIN Mazurka, Op 68, No. 4 (Posth.)

388 MOZART Piano Sonata, F Major, K. 280

SCHUBERT Trio, B♭ Major, Op 99

Allegro moderato

390 HAYDN Piano Sonata, F Major, No. 29

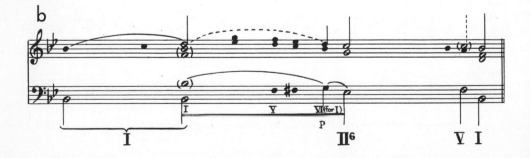

391   SCHUMANN Forest Scenes, No. 6

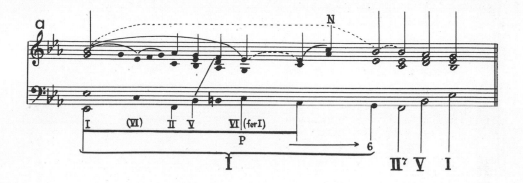

392   BACH Chorale (No. 5)

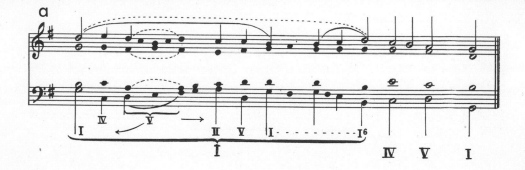

CHOPIN Waltz, Op 64, No. 2

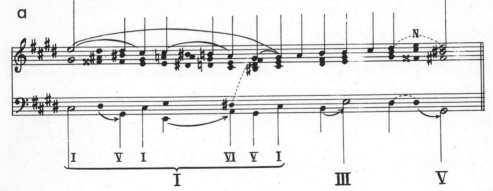

a

b

SCHUBERT Piano Sonata, B♭ Major

Molto moderato

395

396

397

398

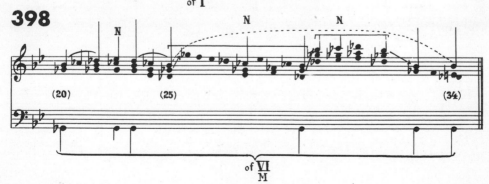

399

400

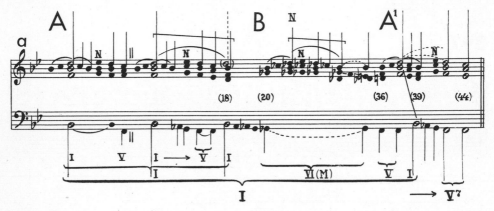

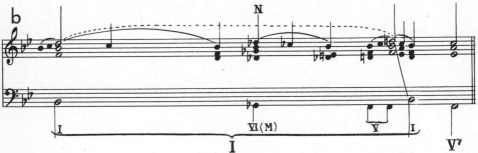

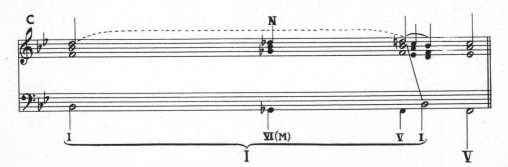

401   HAYDN String Quartet, Op 20, No. 5

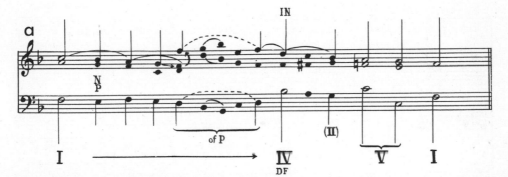

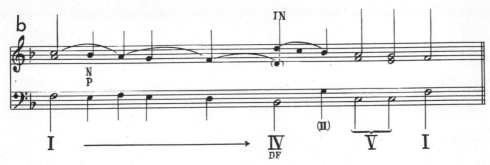

LASSO Motet: Recordare Jesu pie

[From OL, Vol. 15]

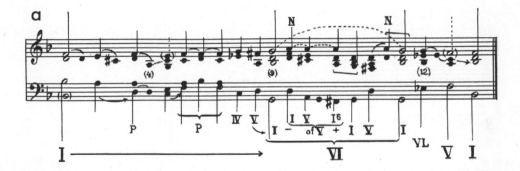

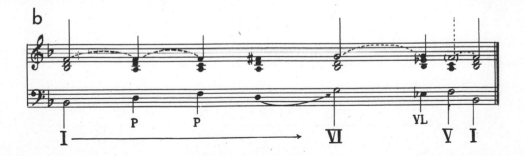

GASTOLDI Balletto: Speme amorosa

[From SHM, No. 20]

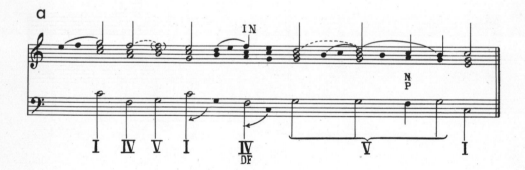

a

I IV V I IV V I
        DF

b

(1-4) (5-8)

WAGNER "Tristan und Isolde"
(Act II)

Nun führst du in dein Ei - - gen, dein Er - - be mir zu

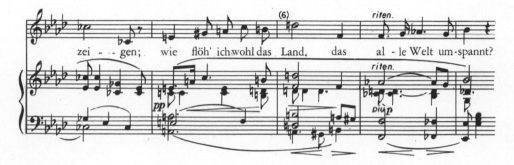

zei - - gen; wie flöh' ich wohl das Land, das al - le Welt um - spannt?

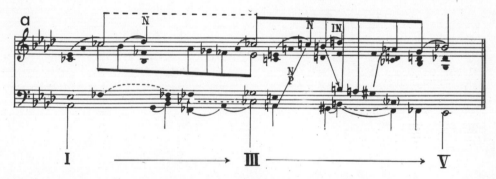

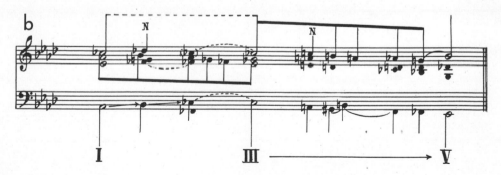

FRANCK Prelude, Aria and Finale

Allegro moderato e maestoso

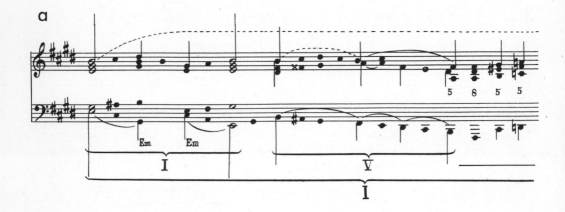

a

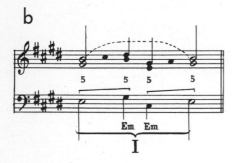

b

a cont'd

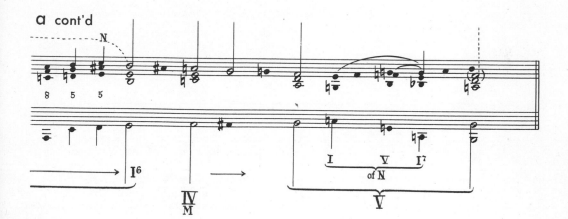

c

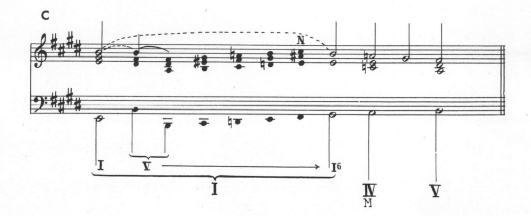

R. STRAUSS Quintet ("Ariadne auf Naxos")

Leggiero e grazioso

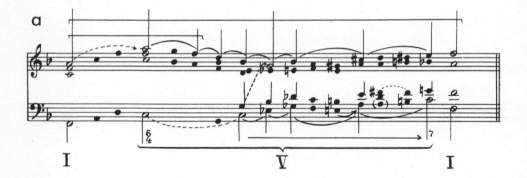

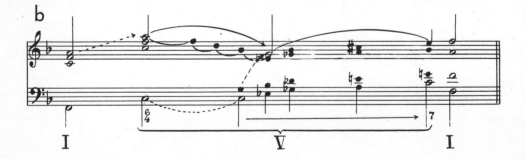

407 R. STRAUSS Quintet ("Ariadne auf Naxos")

Poco tranquillo

a

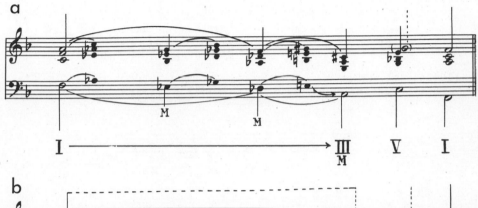

b

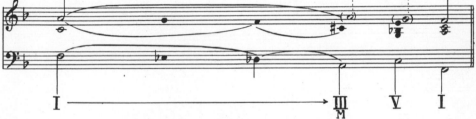

408 BIZET Seguidilla ("Carmen," Act I)

Allegretto

Près des\rem-parts de Sé-vil----le,

Chez _ mon a - mi _ Lil - las Pas - tia _ J'i -

rai dan - ser la Sé - gue - dille Et boi - re du Man - za - nil - la _

_ J'i - rai chez mon a - mi Lil - las Pas - tia. _

409 CHOPIN Polonaise-Fantasy

a

a

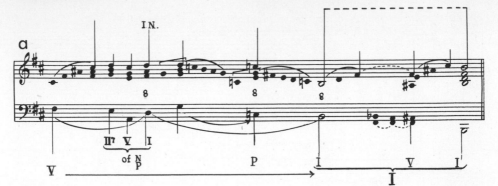

b

c

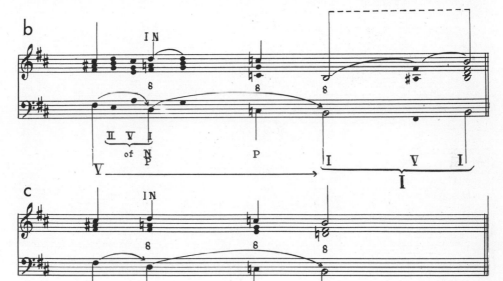

a cont'd

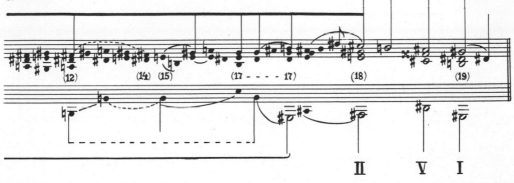

b

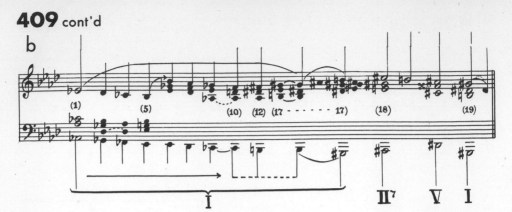

c

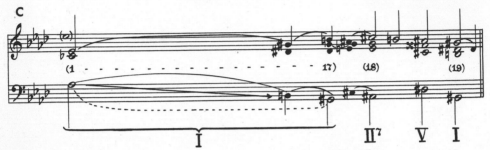

d

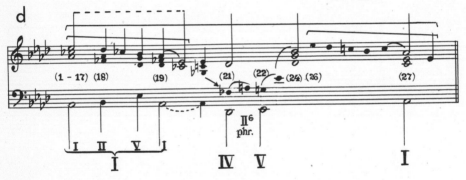

e

f

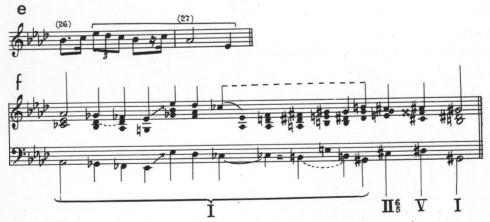

410 HINDEMITH Piano Sonata No. 2.

Lively

a

b

c

411 MARTINŮ Sonata for Cello and Piano No. 2.

412 COPLAND 3 Excerpts from "Our Town," No. 1

a

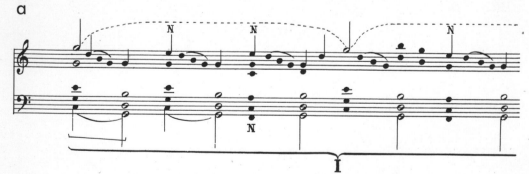

411 cont'd

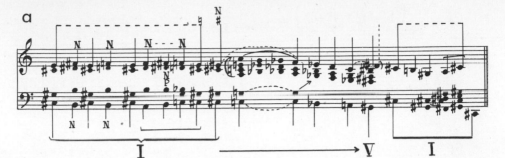

a

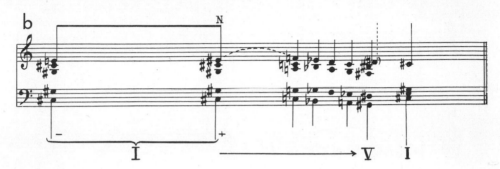

b

412 cont'd

a cont'd

413 WAGENAAR Ciacona

a

b **c**

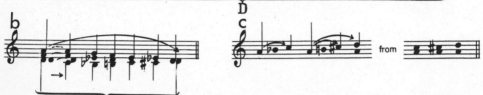

414 MARTINŮ Sonata for Violin and Piano No. 2

a

RAVEL Jeux d'eau

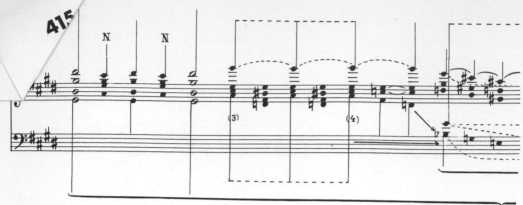

b

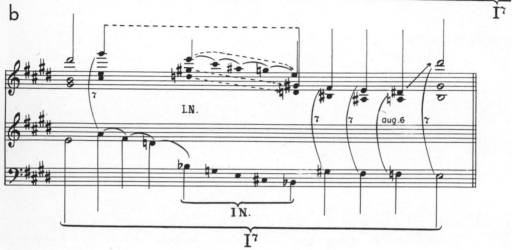

416 COPLAND Piano Sonata

415 cont'd

a cont'd

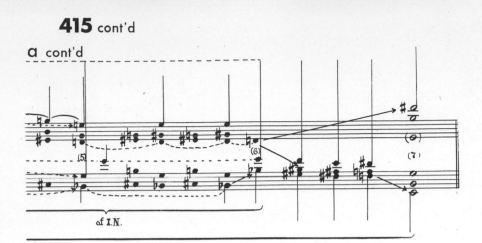

of I.N.

c

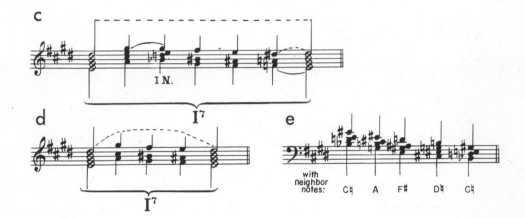

I N.

I^7

d

I^7

e

with
neighbor
notes: C♮ A F♯ D♮ C♮

416 cont'd

a

a cont'd

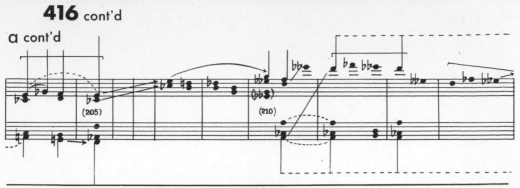

F(V)

a cont'd

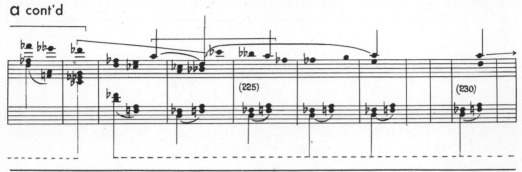

F(V)

b

F(V)
polychord

d

417 STRAVINSKY Symphony in Three Movements

418 BARTOK Bagatelle Op 6, No. 4

419 R. STRAUSS "Elektra"

Copyright 1908 by Boosey & Hawkes, Ltd.; used by special permission.

420 BEETHOVEN Piano Concerto No. 4, G Major

a

I V I⁶

I   II   V   (substitute for I)   I   II⁶ V I
         (D)

421

a

b

c

o7

422

a

b

423

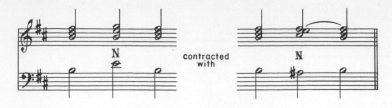

424 BACH Cantata: Du wahrer Gott und Davids Sohn

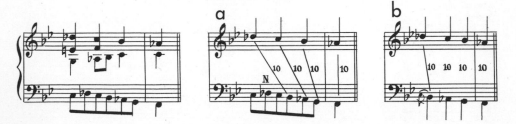

425 SCHUMANN Romance, Op 28, No. 1

426 COUPERIN La Favorite

a

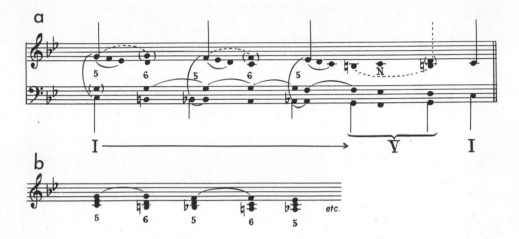

b

etc.

427 BYRD Sacerdotes Domini

a

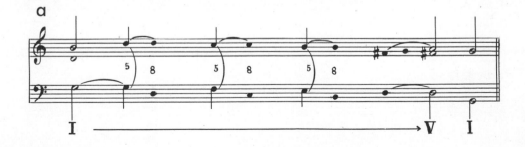

428 MOUSSORGSKY Ballet of the Unhatched Chickens (Pictures from an Exhibition)

429 VERDI Oro supplex (Requiem)

430 BEETHOVEN Piano Sonata,
C Major, Op 53. Introduzione

431 CHOPIN Polonaise, Op 26

431 cont'd

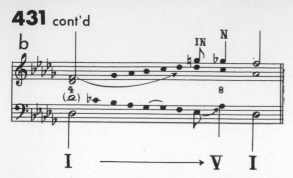

I ———————————→ V I

432 CHOPIN Mazurka, Op 59, No. 2

a

I ———————————————————————→

b

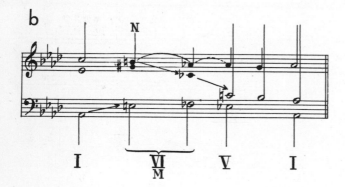

I $\frac{VI}{M}$ V I

431 cont'd

c

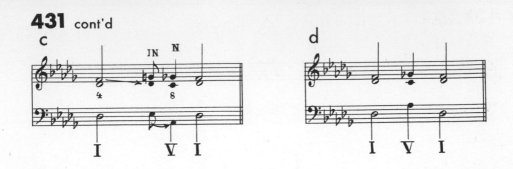

I V I   d   I V I

432 cont'd

a cont'd

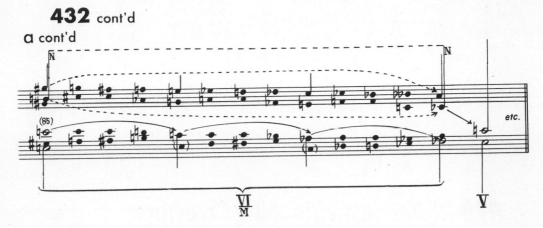

VI / M V

433 CHOPIN Polonaise, Op 40

a

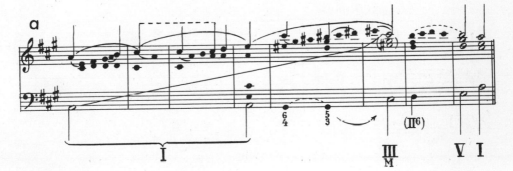

I III / M V I

434

Instead of 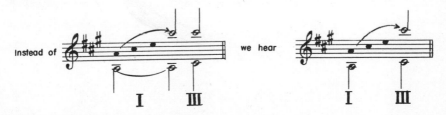 we hear

I III   I III

FARNABY A Toye

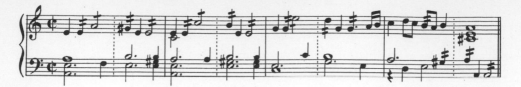

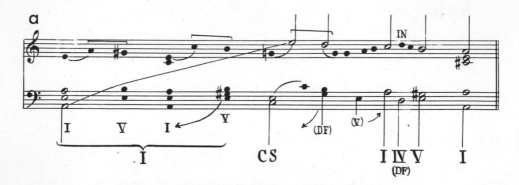

436 ## MENDELSSOHN Overture, "A Midsummer Night's Dream"

437   SCHUBERT Piano Sonata, C minor

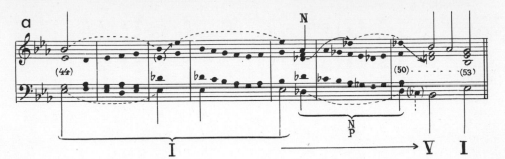

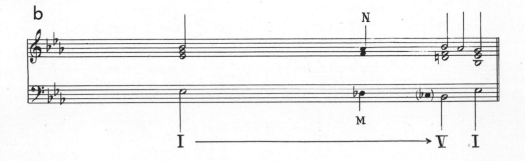

438   SCHUBERT Fantasia-Sonata

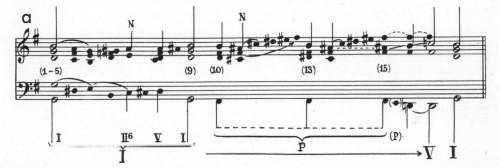

439 SCHUMANN Piano Quintet

Allegro brillante

a

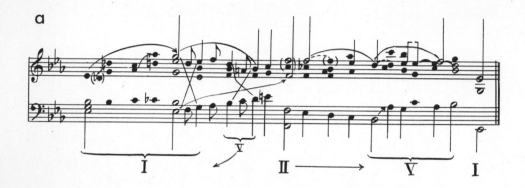

441 BARTÓK From 10 Easy Pieces for Piano

Poco andante

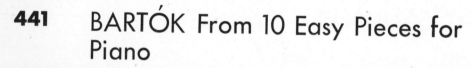

a

439 cont'd

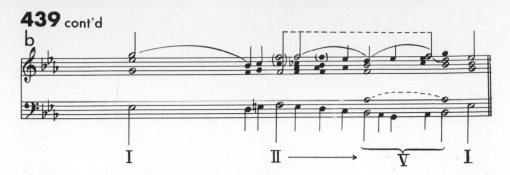

I   II ⟶   Ⅴ   I

440 BEETHOVEN Piano Sonata,
G Major, Op 31, No. 1

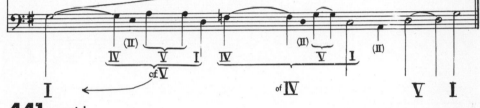

441 cont'd

a cont'd

442

a

BEETHOVEN Piano Sonata,
F minor, Op 2, No. 1

443

a

BEETHOVEN Piano Sonata,
C minor, Op 10, No. 1.

444

a

MOZART Piano Sonata, C Major,
K. 279

a cont'd

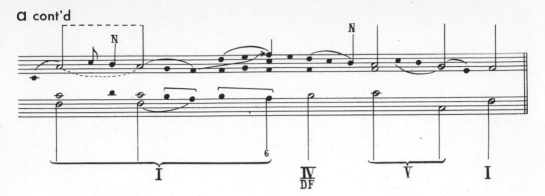

b

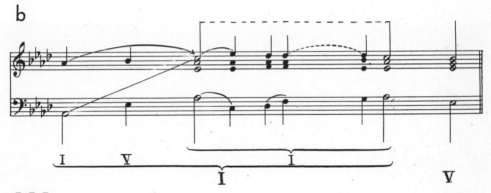

a cont'd

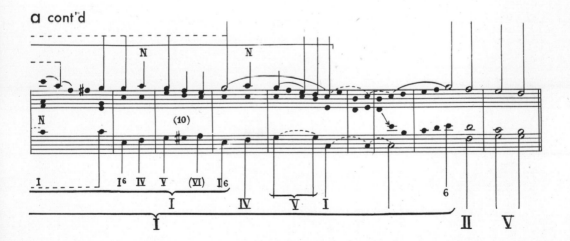

MAHLER Kindertotenlieder, No. 1

a

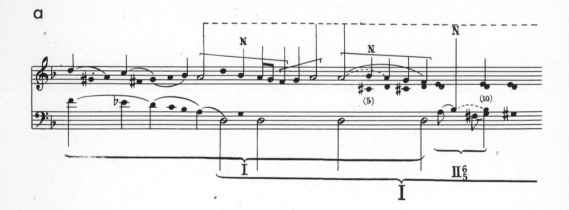

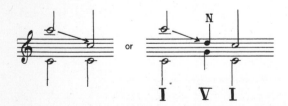

Un - glück, kein Un - glück die Nacht ge - scheh'n!

a cont'd

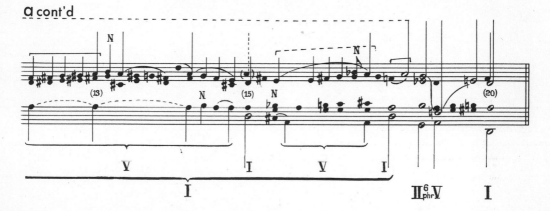

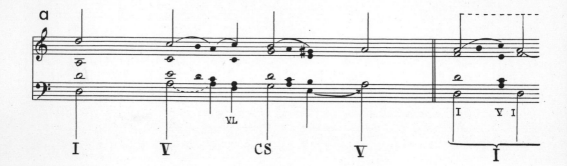

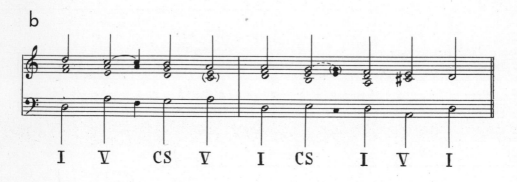

[From MET, No. 39]

a cont'd

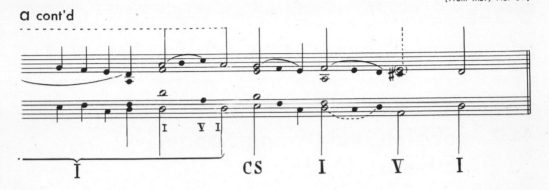

I   Ⅴ   I

I   CS   I   Ⅴ   I

448   SCHUBERT Die Krähe

a

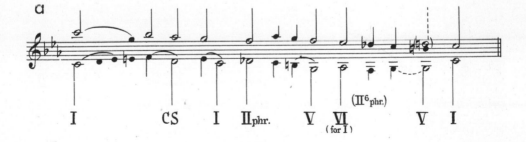

I   CS   I   Ⅱphr.   Ⅴ   Ⅵ   (Ⅱ⁶phr.)   Ⅴ   I
                           (for I)

449 RAMEAU Choeur des Spartiates
("Castor et Pollux," Act I)

450 BEETHOVEN Piano Sonata,
E minor, Op 90

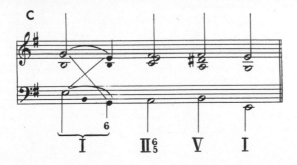

451 PROKOFIEFF Piano Sonata No. 8, Op 84

a

b

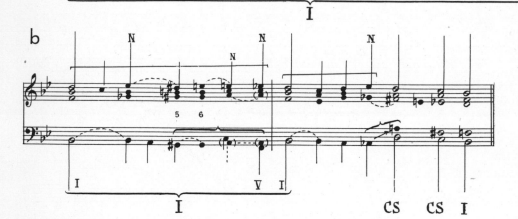

c

451 cont'd

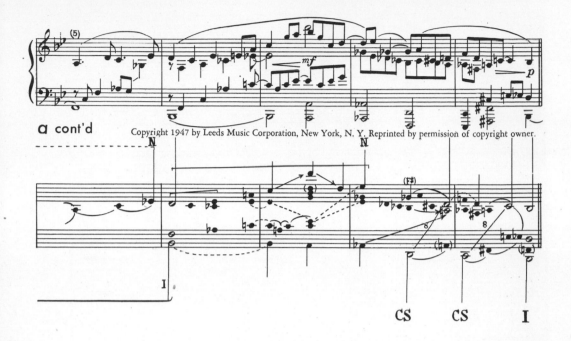

a cont'd

452 BARTOK String Quartet No. 5

Adagio molto

Un poco più Andante

a

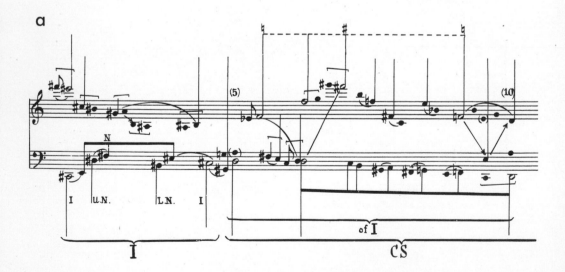

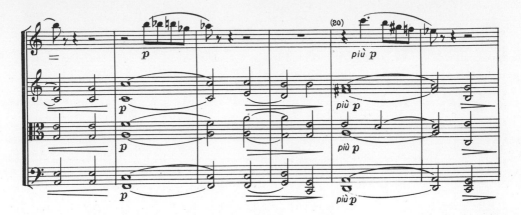

a cont'd

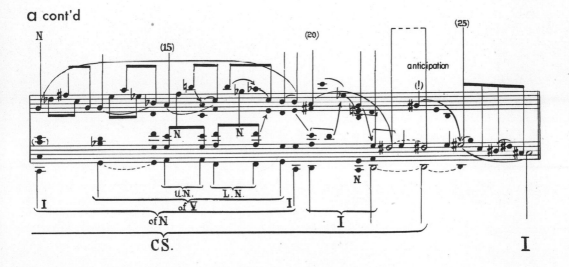

b

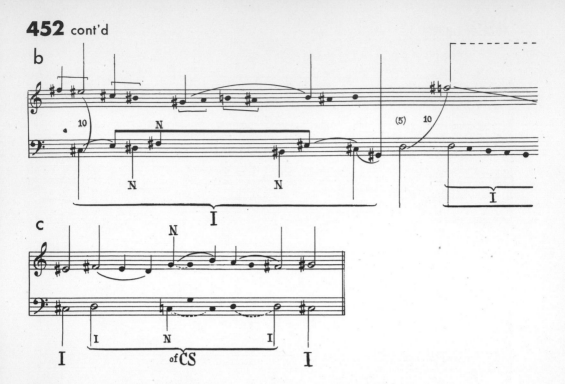

c

453   HINDEMITH Piano Sonata No. 1

With quiet motion, in quarters

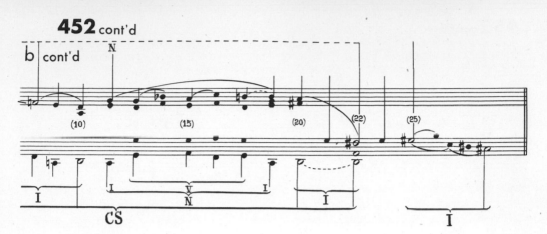

452 cont'd

453 cont'd

Copyright 1936 by Associated Music Publishers, Inc.; used by special permission.

a

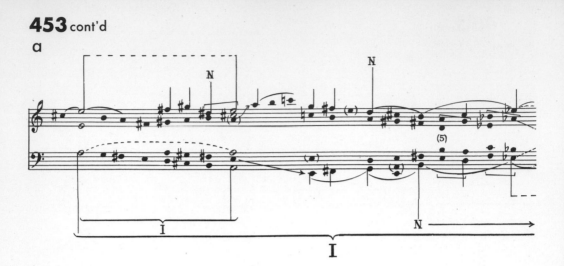

a cont'd

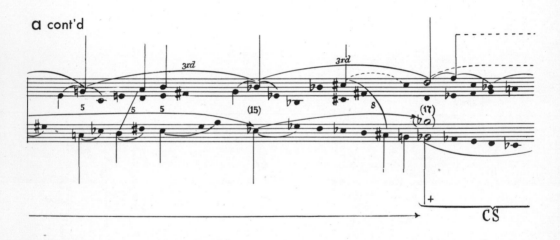

b

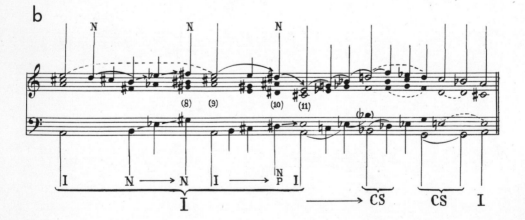

a cont'd

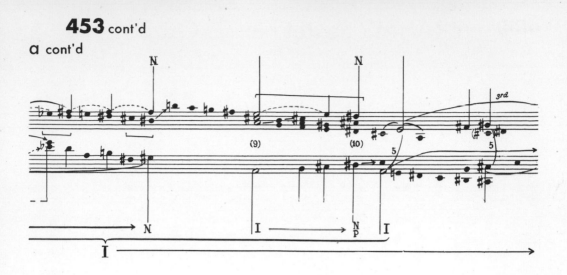

a cont'd

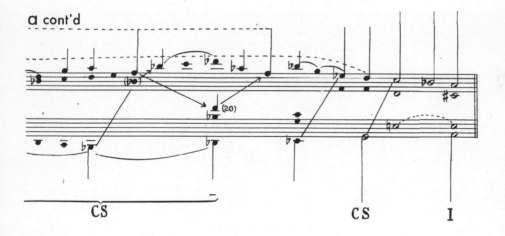

c

a

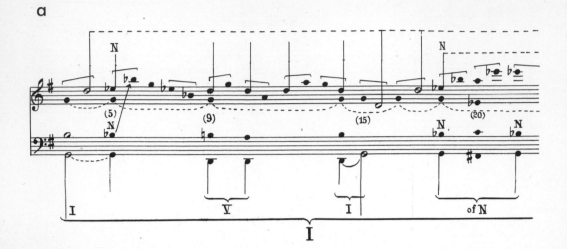

a cont'd

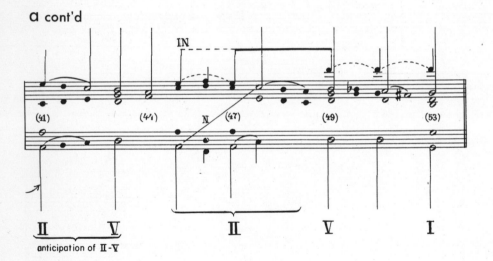

anticipation of II-V

a cont'd

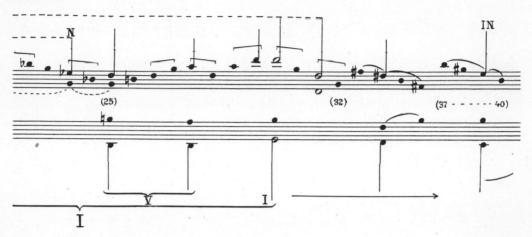

b

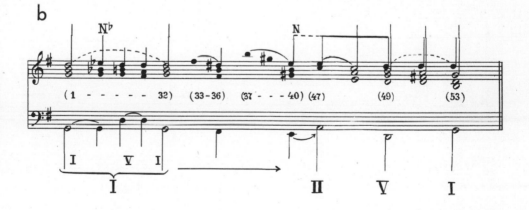

DEBUSSY Prélude à l'après-midi
d'un faune

a

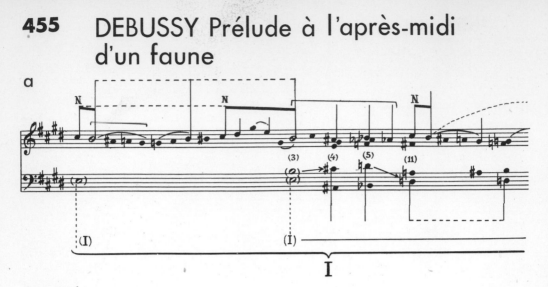

a cont'd

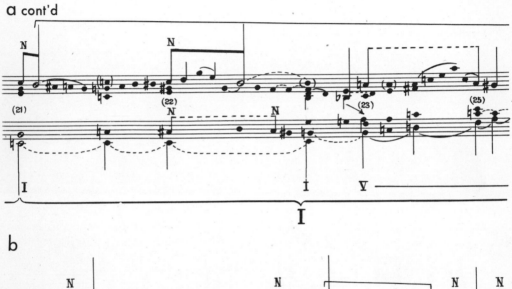

b

a cont'd

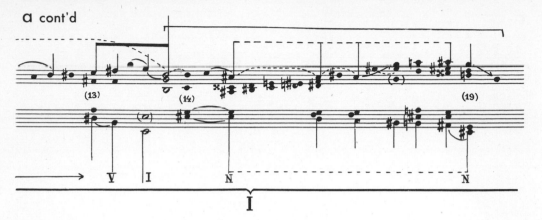

a cont'd

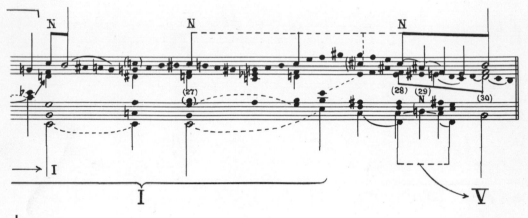

b cont'd

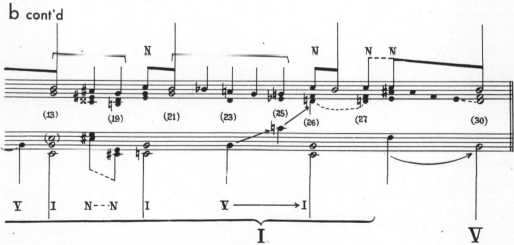

456 **CHOPIN** Nocturne, Op 48, No. 2

a

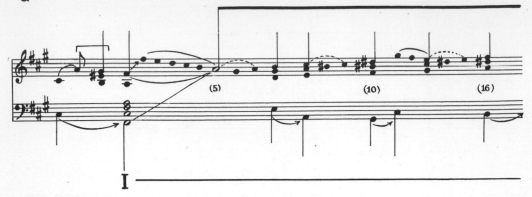

(5)   (10)   (16)

I

b

I ⟶ II♯ V
         M

457 **PROKOFIEFF** Piano Sonata No. 3

a

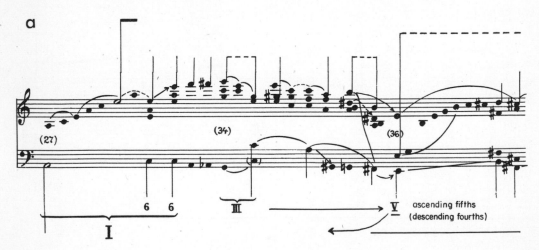

(27)   (34)   (36)

6 6   III ⟶ V   ascending fifths
                 (descending fourths)
I

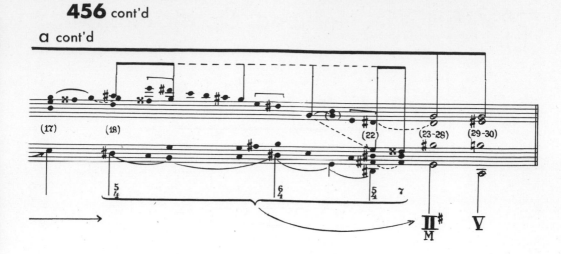

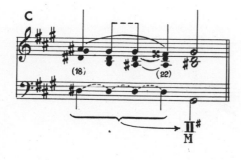

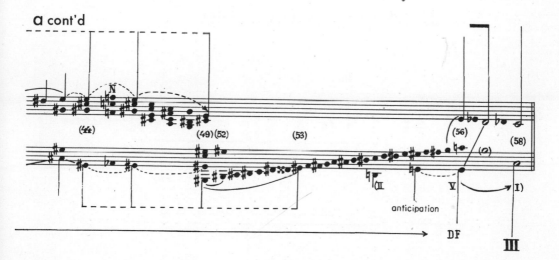

b

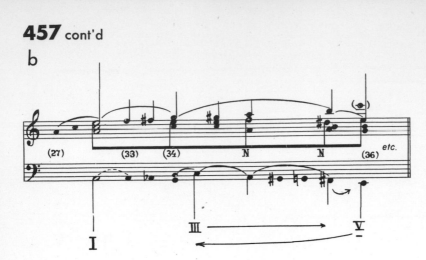

d

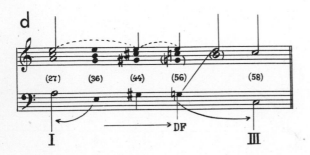

458 BEETHOVEN Piano Sonata,
D Major, Op 10, No. 3

a

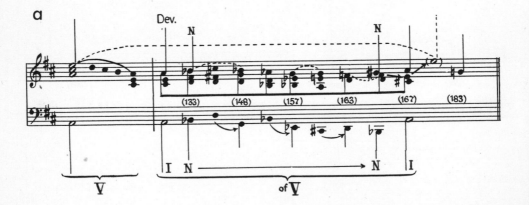

457 cont'd

c

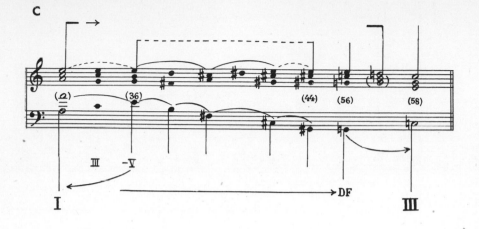

458 cont'd

b

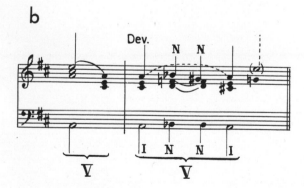

HAYDN Symphony D Major,
No. 104

a

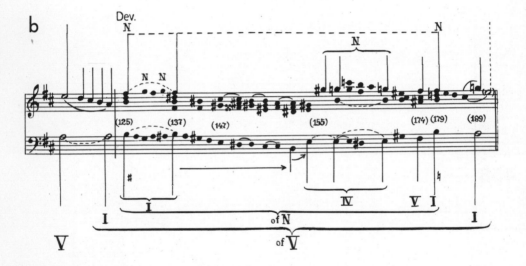

b

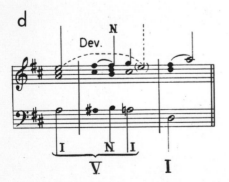

d

a cont'd

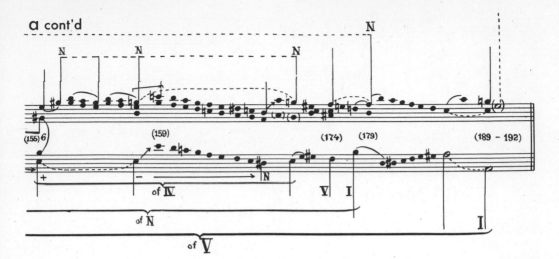

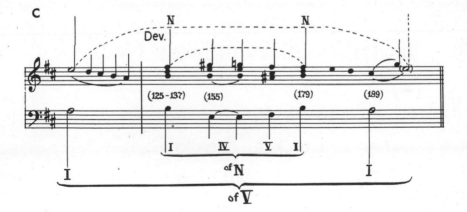

460

a

I   IV

b

I   IV

6   6   6

461 BEETHOVEN Piano Sonata,
B♭ Major, Op 22

a

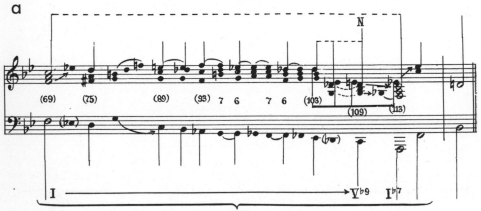

N

(69) (75) (89) (93) 7 6 7 6 (103)

(109) (113)

I ⟶ V♭9 I♭7

of V

462 BEETHOVEN Symphony No. 7

a

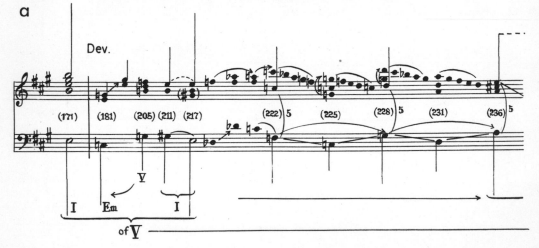

Dev.

(171) (181) (205)(211)(217) (222) 5 (225) (228) 5 (231) (236) 5

V

I Em I

of V

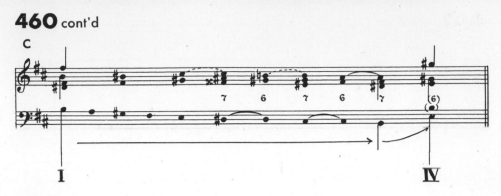

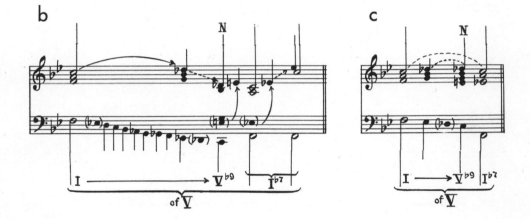

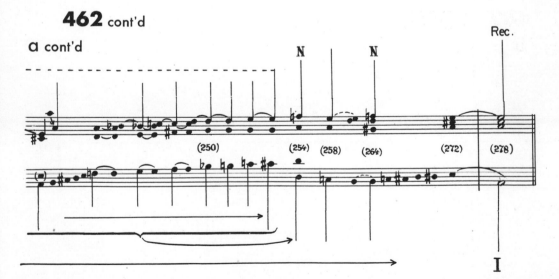

b

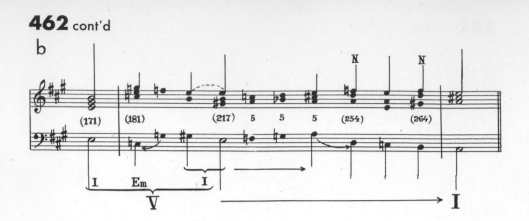

463 BEETHOVEN Piano Sonata,
C minor, Op 10, No. 1

a

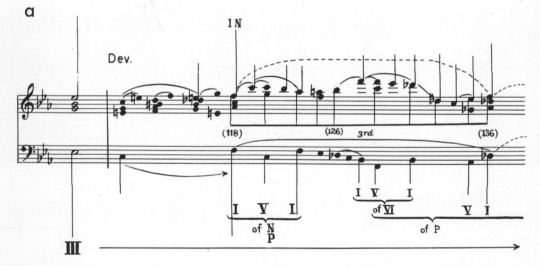

b

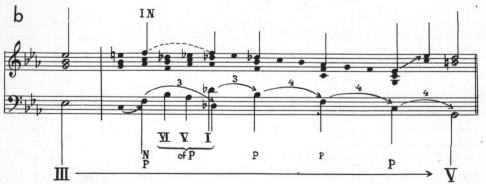

462 cont'd

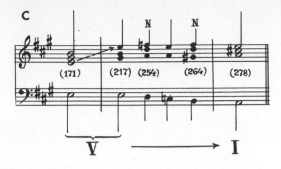

463 cont'd

a cont'd

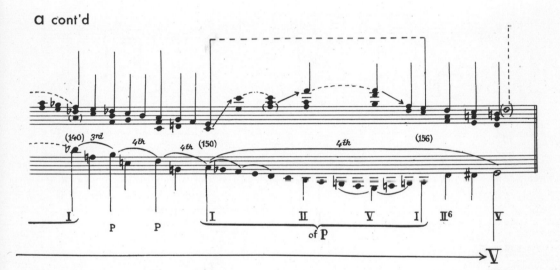

c

d

BEETHOVEN Piano Sonata, F minor, Op 57

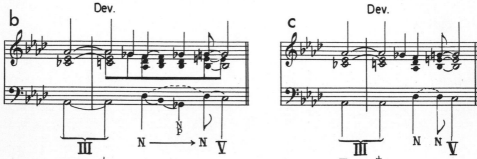

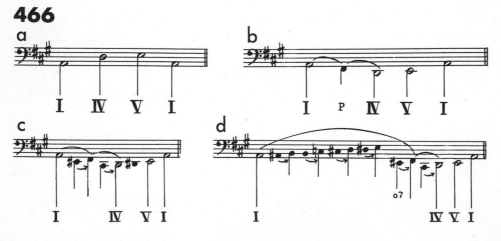

467

468

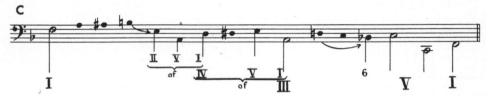

469

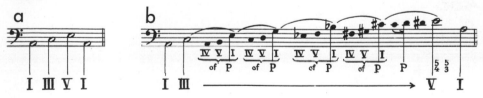

470

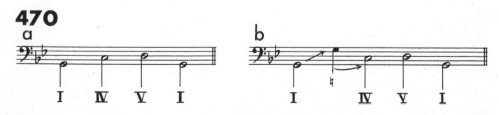

470 cont'd

c

471 WAGNER "Parsifal," (Act I)

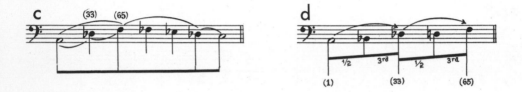

a   b

c   d

e

g cont'd

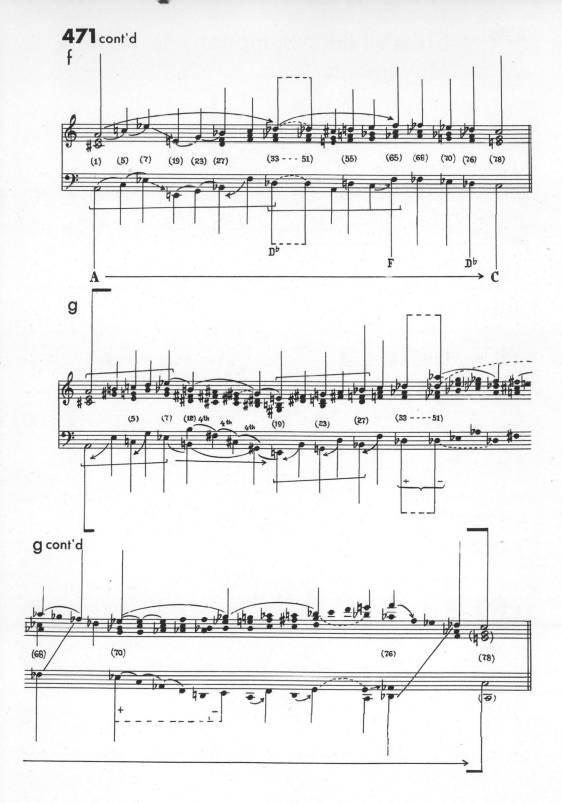

STRAVINSKY Symphony in Three Movements

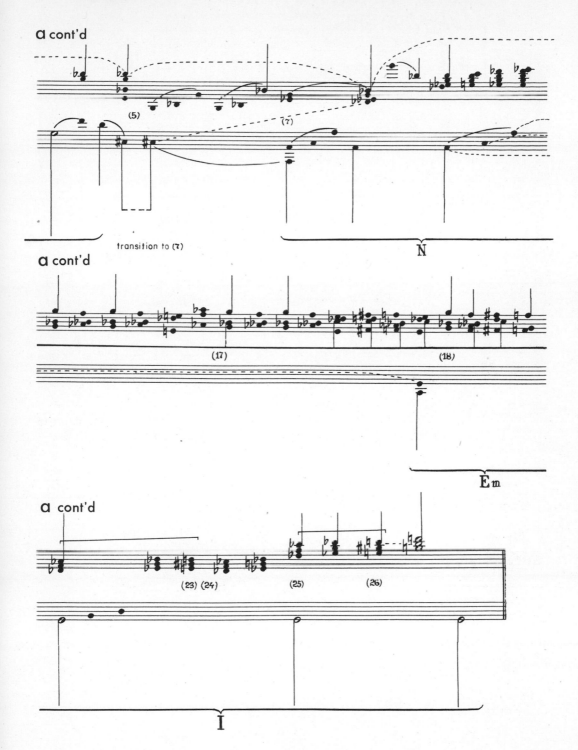

b

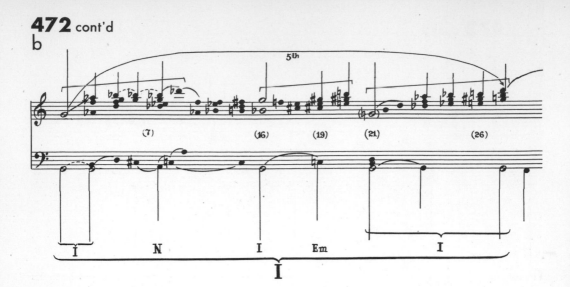

c

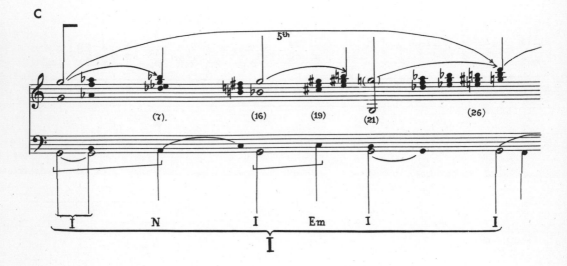

d

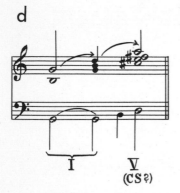

b cont'd

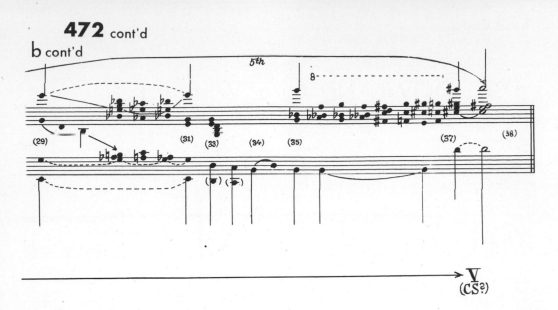

c cont'd

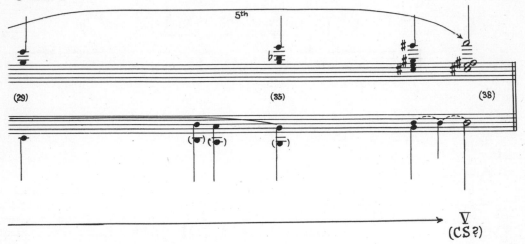

473 DOWLAND Ayre: What if I
never speed

[From *HAM*, Vol. I, No. 163]

a

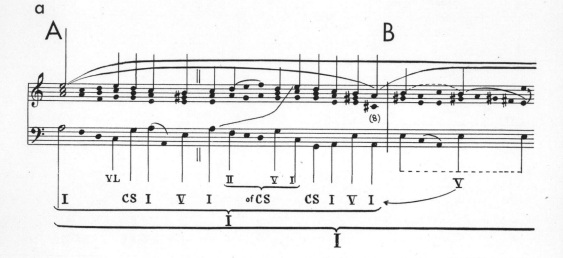

b

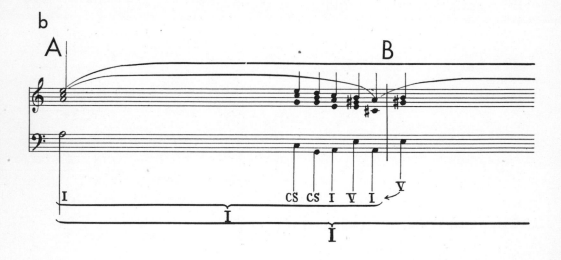

a cont'd

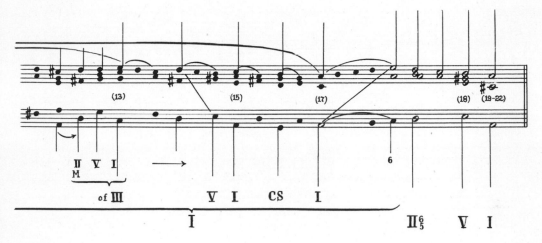

b cont'd

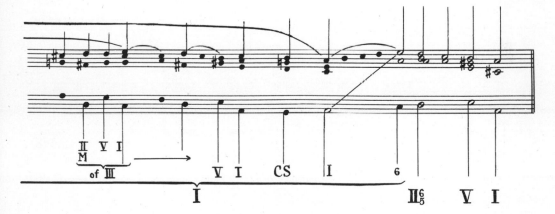

a

a cont'd

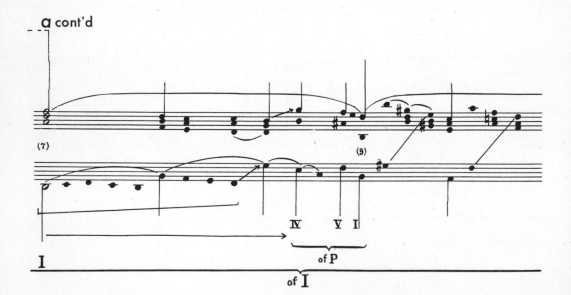

a cont'd

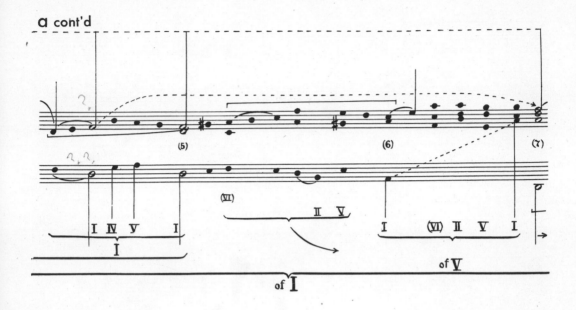

a cont'd

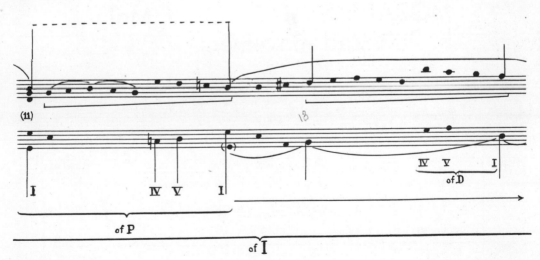

475 MOZART Piano Sonata, F Major, K. 280. 2nd movement

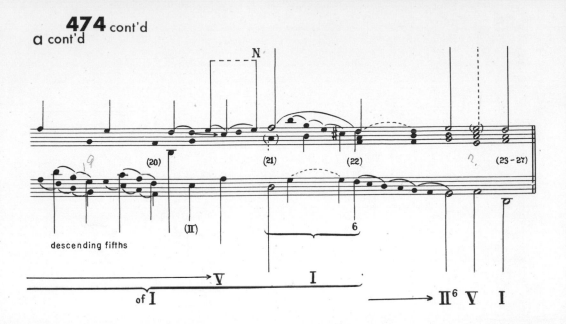

descending fifths

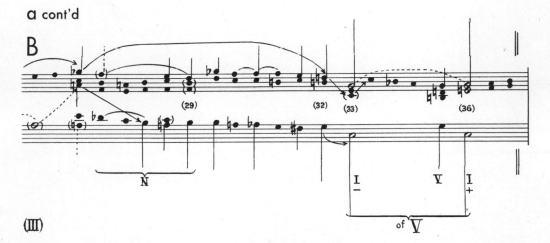

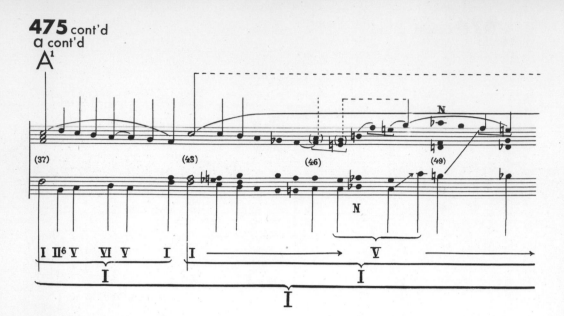

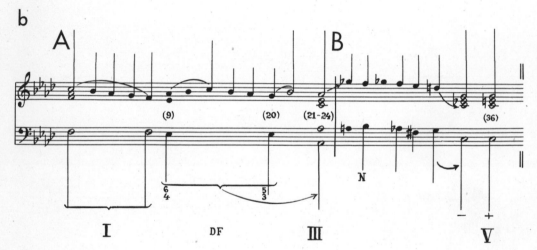

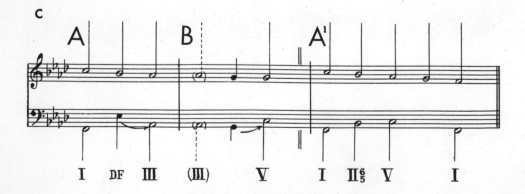

475 cont'd

a cont'd

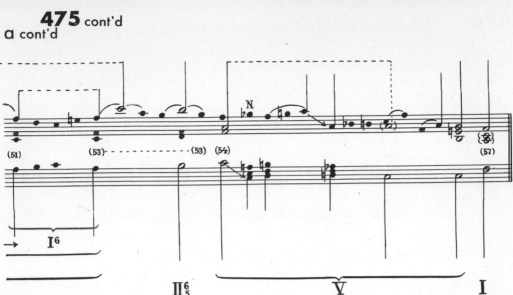

b cont'd

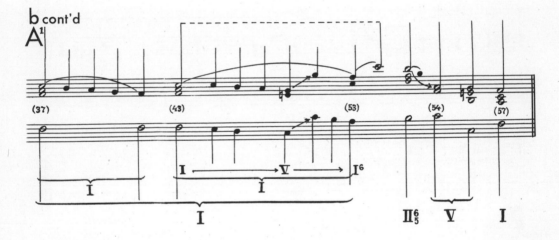

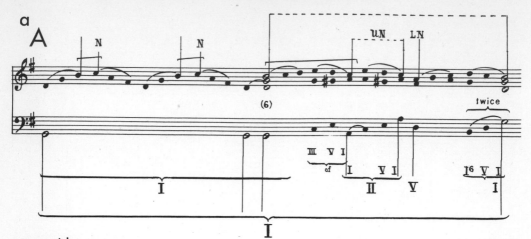

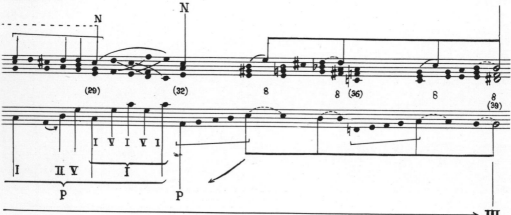

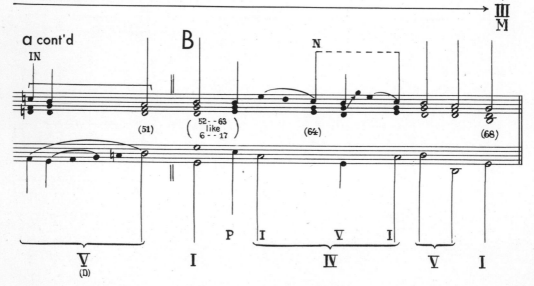

a cont'd

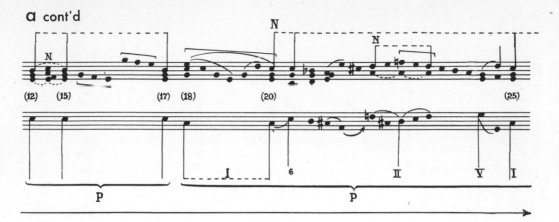

a cont'd

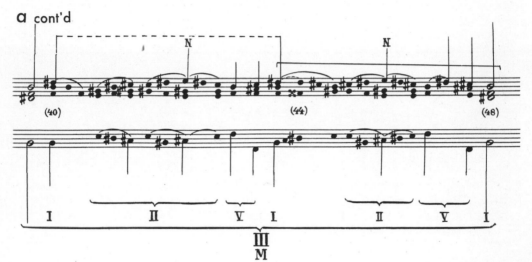

b

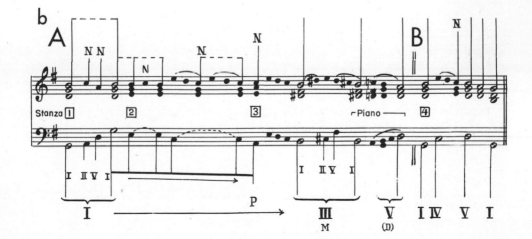

477 BRAHMS Intermezzo, Op. 119, No. 1

a

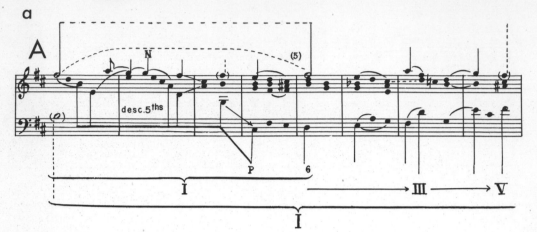

a cont'd

B

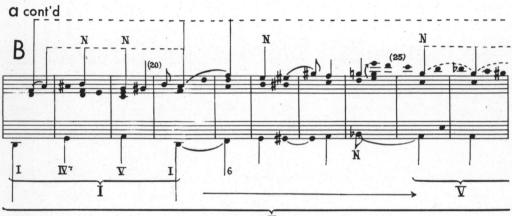

a cont'd

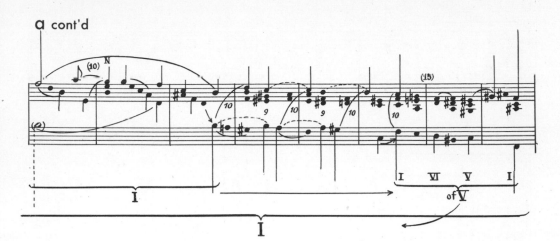

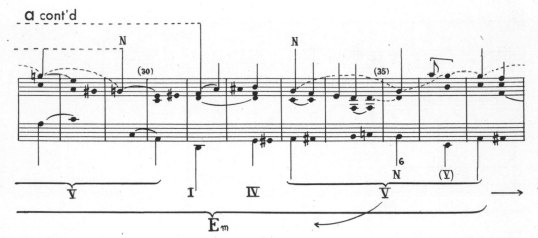

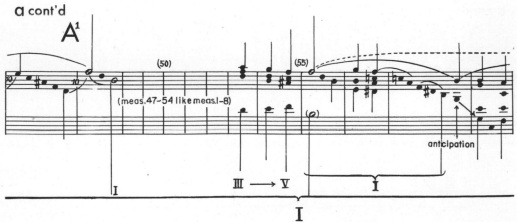

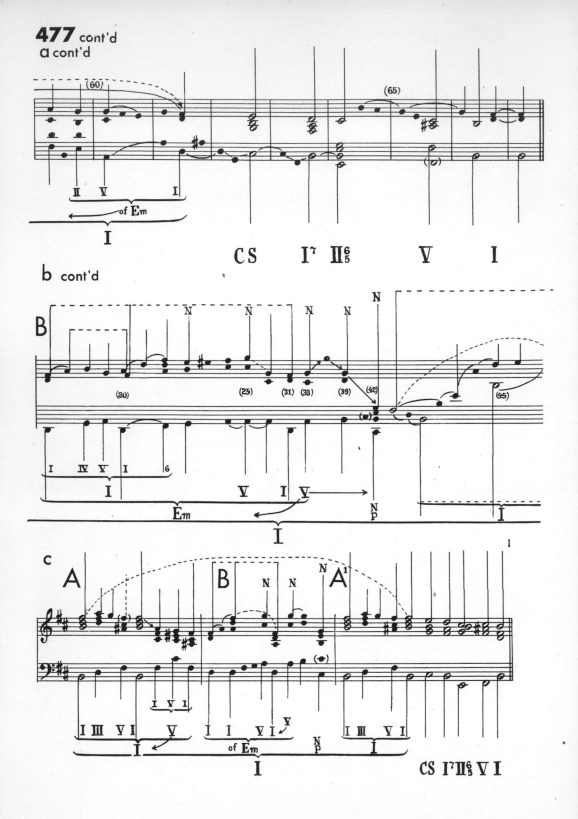

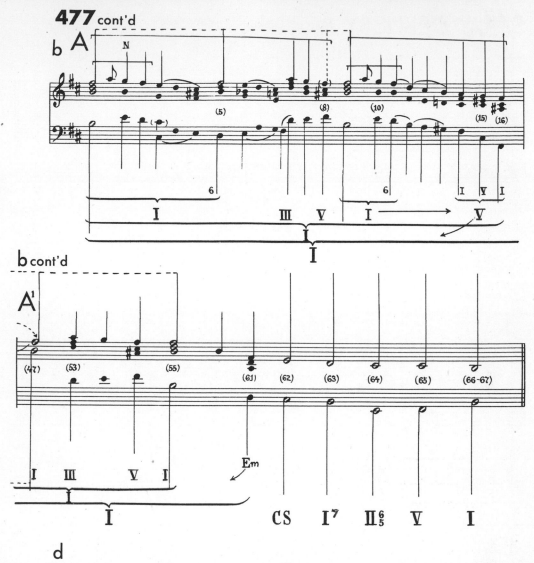

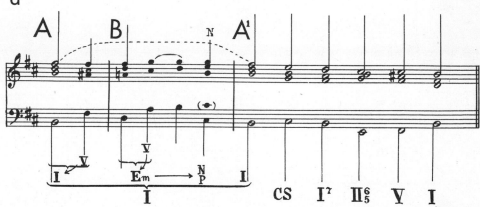

DEBUSSY Bruyères

a

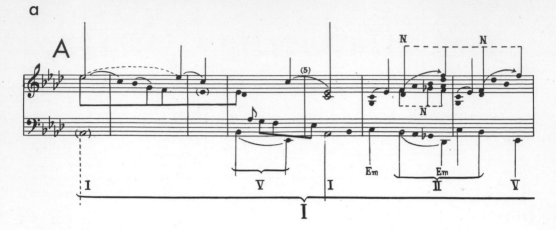

a cont'd

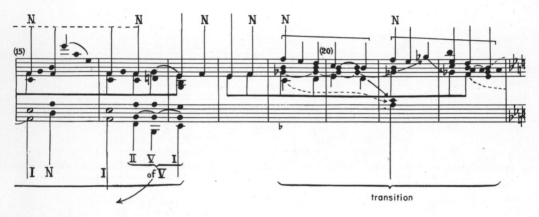

a cont'd

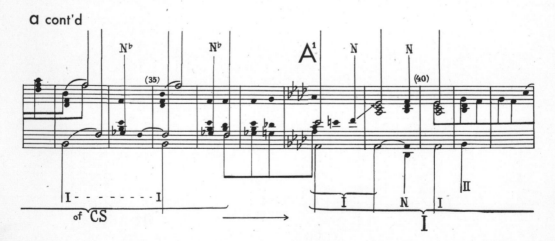

a cont'd

a cont'd

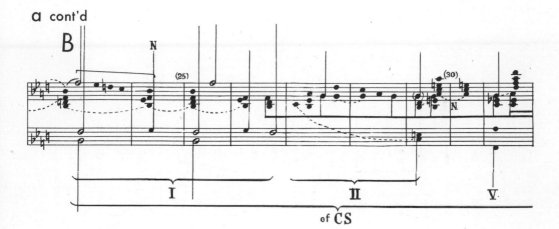

a cont'd

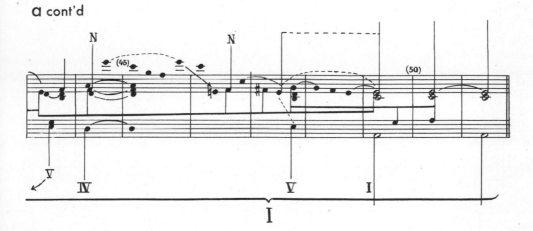

b

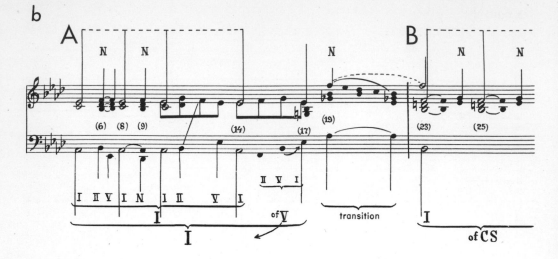

c

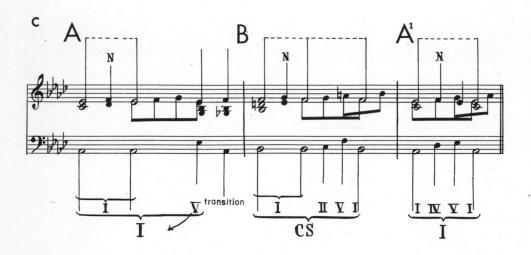

d

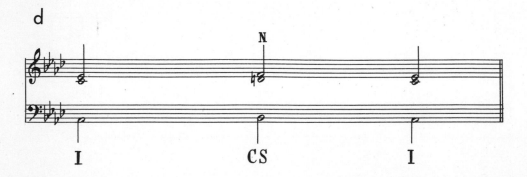

b cont'd

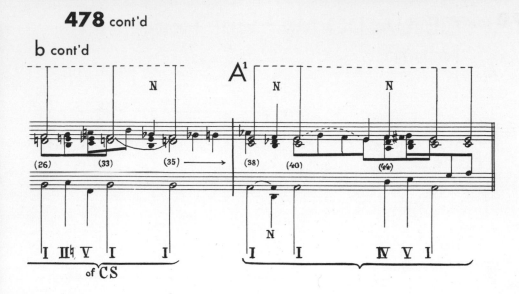

e

Melodic prolongations:

479 GESUALDO Madrigal: Io pur respiro

[From HAM, Vol. I, No. 161]

a

a cont'd

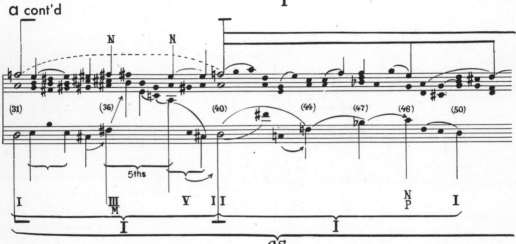

b

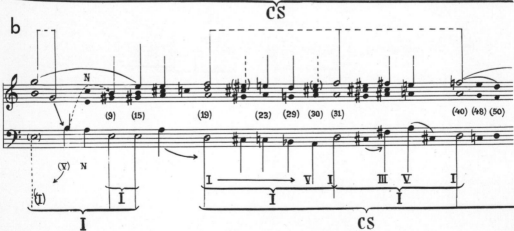

a cont'd

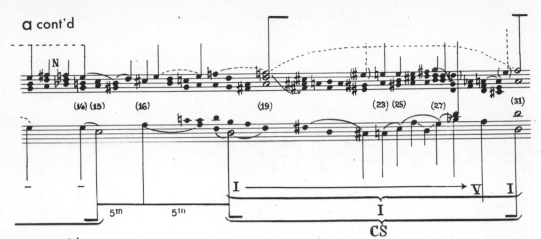

(14) (15) (16)   (19)   (23) (25)   (27)   (31)

I ──────────────────────────→ V   I

I

CS

5ᵗʰ   5ᵗʰ

a cont'd

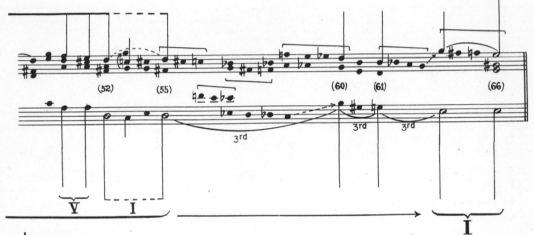

(52)   (55)   (60)   (61)   (66)

3rd   3rd   3rd

V   I ──────────────────────────→

I

b cont'd

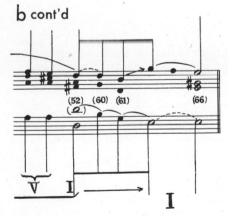

(52) (60) (61)   (66)
(2.)

V   I ───────→

I

c

I   CS   I

a

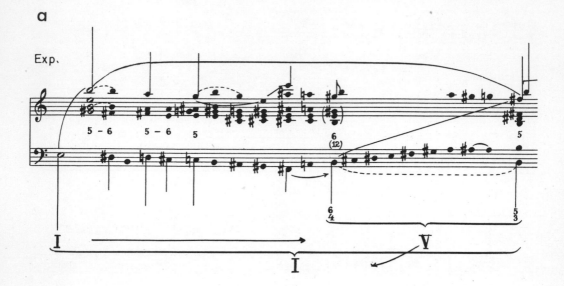

a cont'd

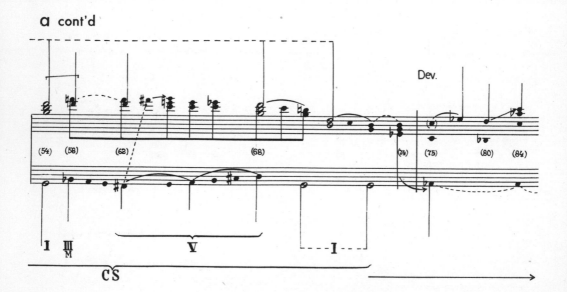

a cont'd

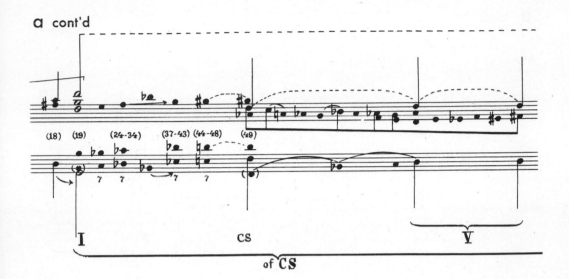

a cont'd

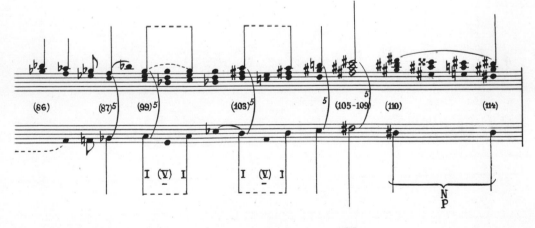

a cont'd

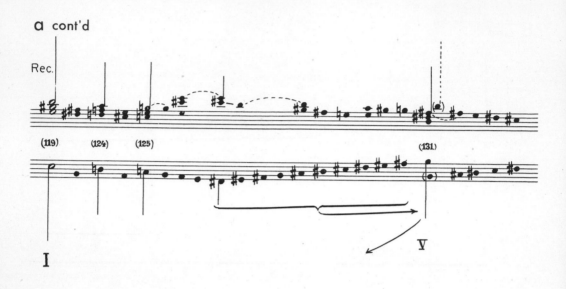

a cont'd

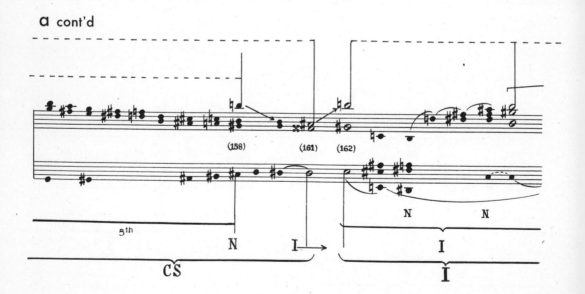

a cont'd

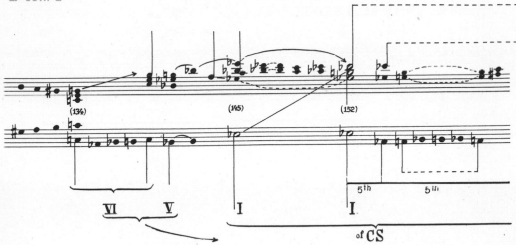

a cont'd

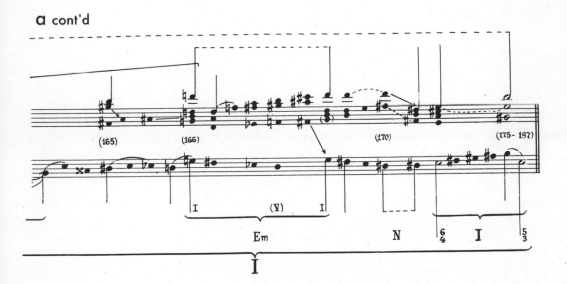

b

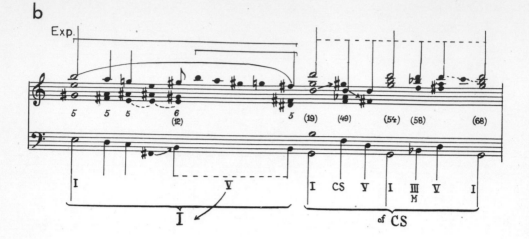

b cont'd

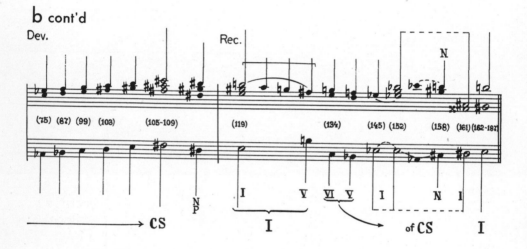

c

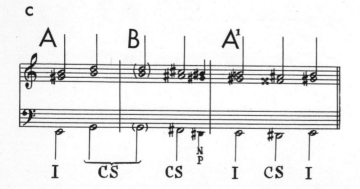

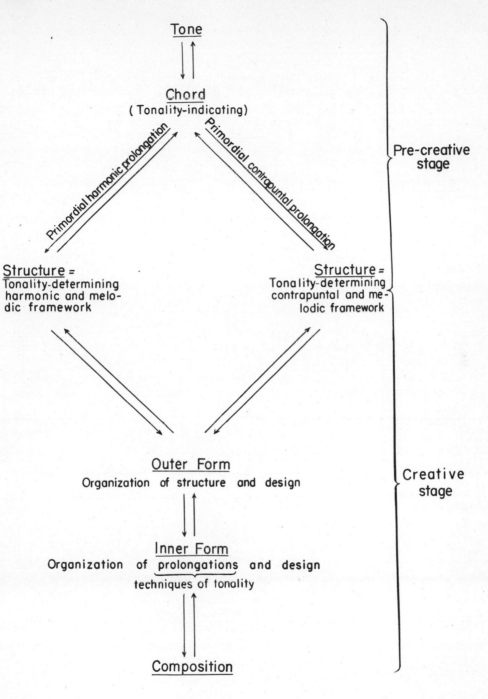

Tone

Chord
(Tonality-indicating)

Primordial harmonic prolongation

Primordial contrapuntal prolongation

Structure =
Tonality-determining
harmonic and melo-
dic framework

Structure =
Tonality-determining
contrapuntal and me-
lodic framework

Outer Form
Organization of structure and design

Inner Form
Organization of prolongations and design
techniques of tonality

Composition

Pre-creative
stage

Creative
stage

[From *SHM*, No. 18]

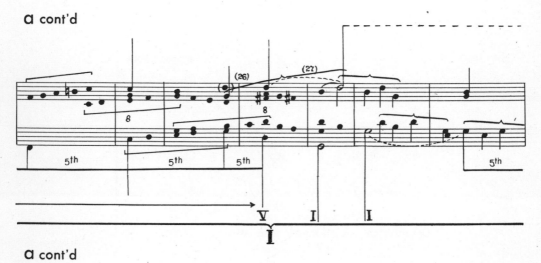

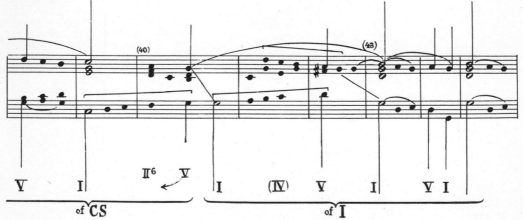

a cont'd

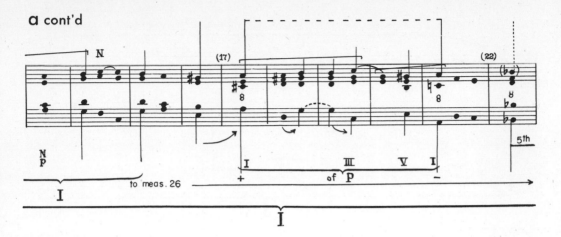

a cont'd

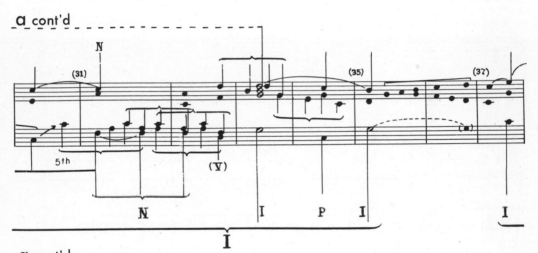

a cont'd

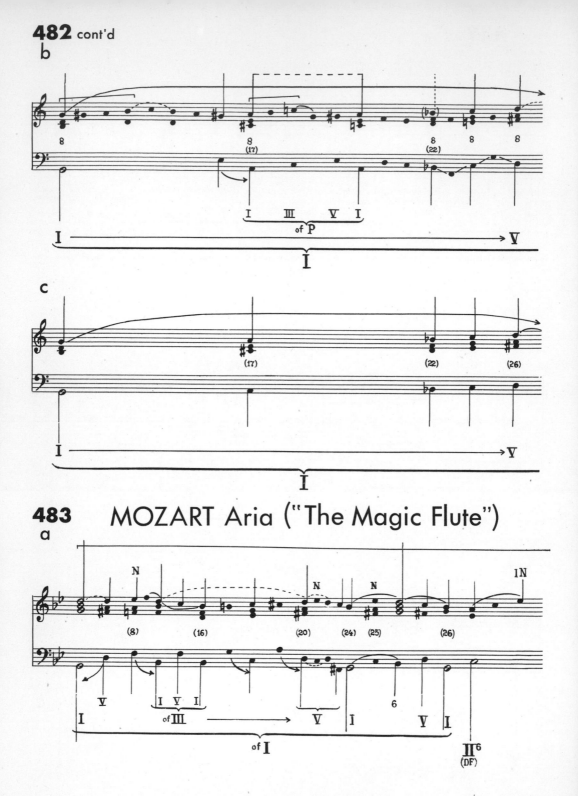

483
a

MOZART Aria ("The Magic Flute")

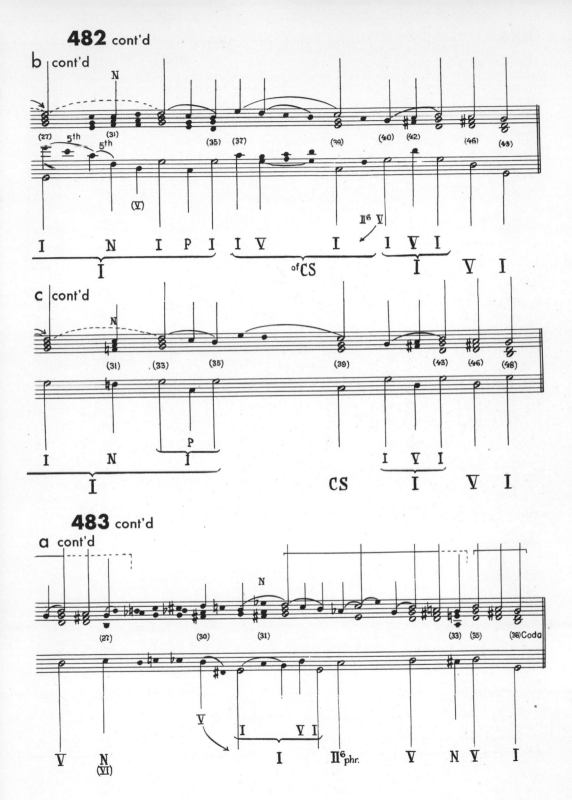

FRESCOBALDI Corrente

[From *AMI*, Vol. III, P. 207]

a

b

485 cont'd

a cont'd

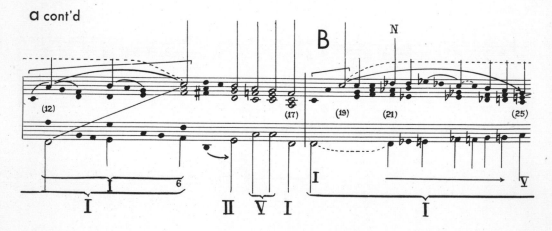

484 cont'd

a cont'd

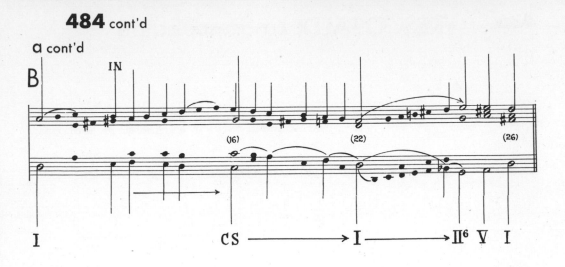

485 BRAHMS Feldeinsamkeit

a

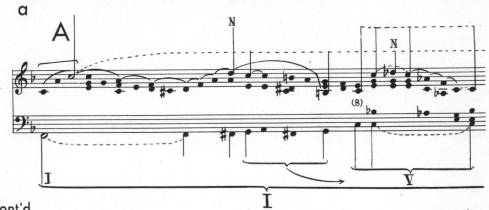

a cont'd

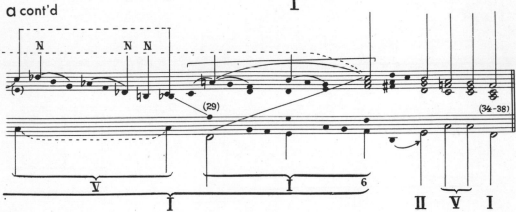

486 FRESCOBALDI La Frescobalda

[From *EPM*, P. 33]

a

b

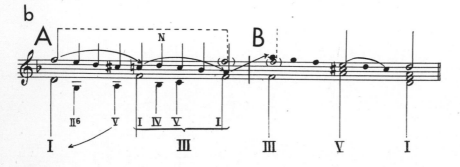

487 D. SCARLATTI Sonata, G Major, L. 490

a

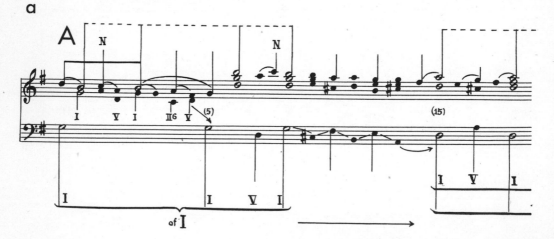

a cont'd

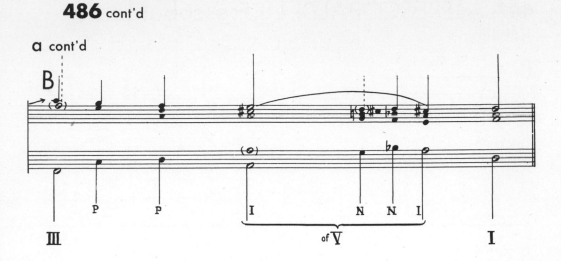

c

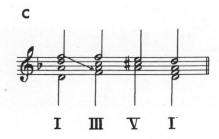

I   III   V   I

487 cont'd

a cont'd

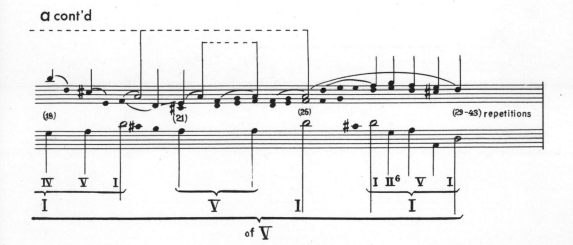

487 cont'd

a cont'd

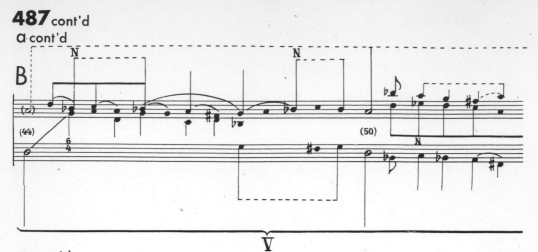

a cont'd

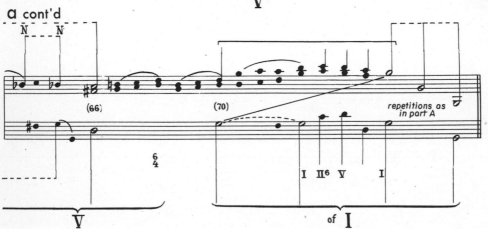

repetitions as in part A

488

a

WOLF In der Frühe

a cont'd

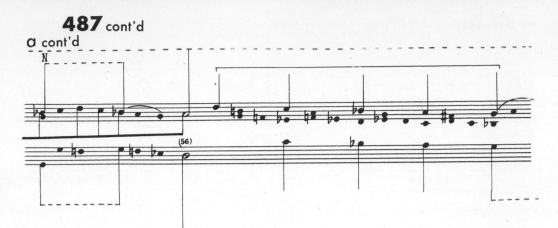

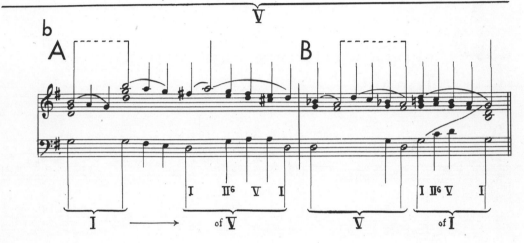

a cont'd

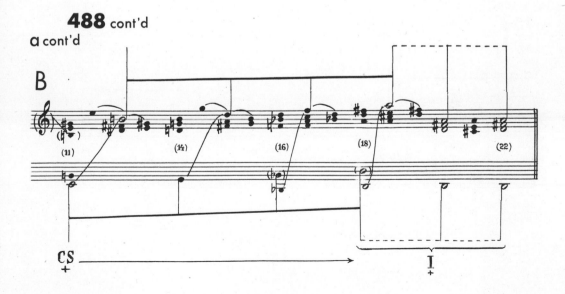

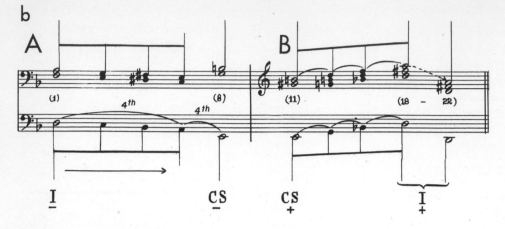

488 cont'd

b

489 # HINDEMITH Interludium (Ludus Tonalis)

a

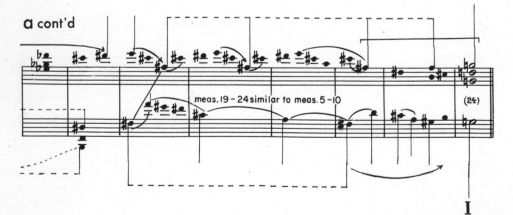

meas.19–24 similar to meas.5–10

489 cont'd

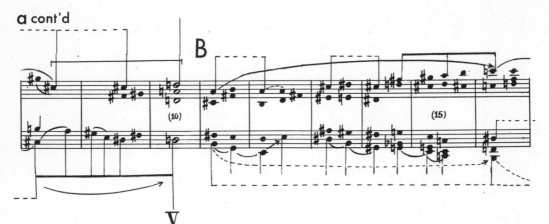

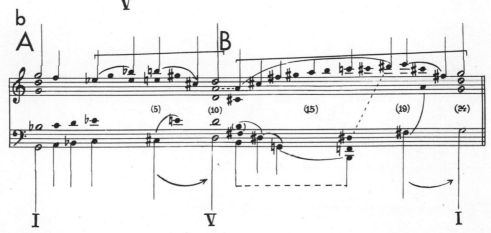

c

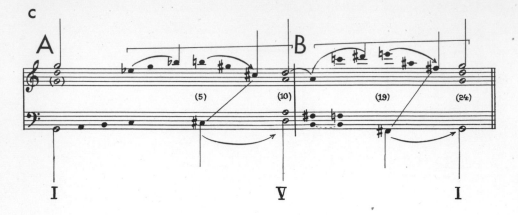

e

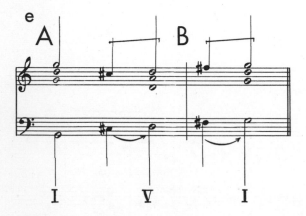

490 BYRD Pavane: The Earle of Salisbury

a

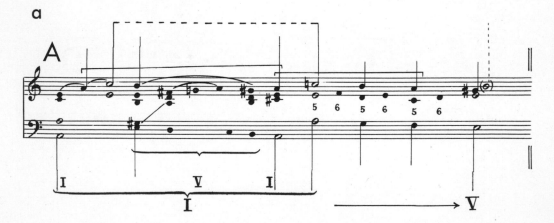

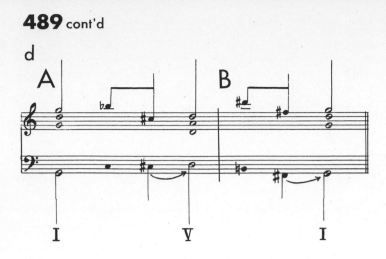

a cont'd

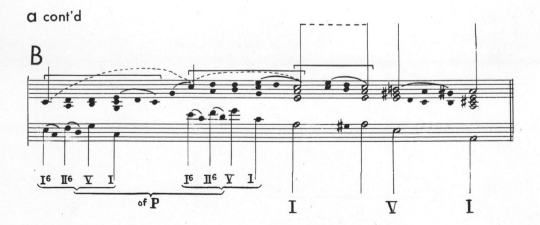

b

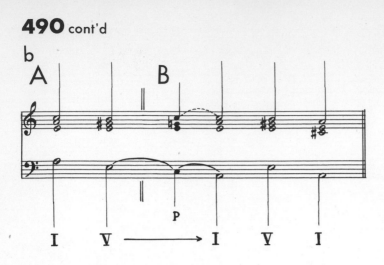

I   V $\longrightarrow$ I   V   I

491 BEETHOVEN String Quartet,
Op 18, No. 5. 3rd movement

a

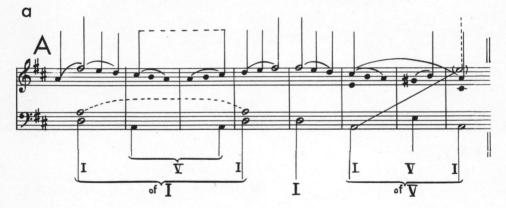

a cont'd

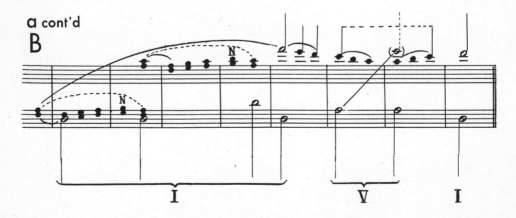

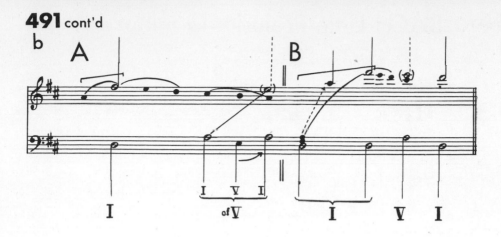

492

CHOPIN Prelude, Op 28, No. 1

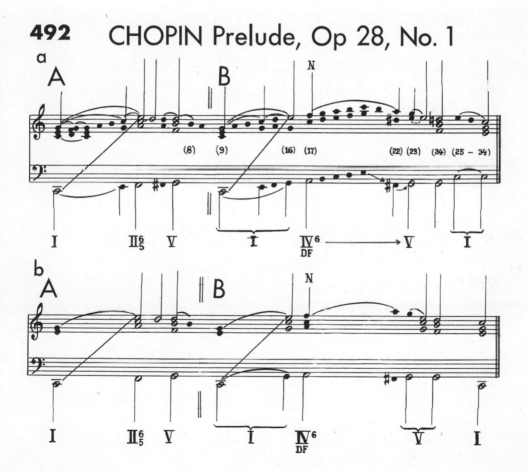

493 BACH Little Prelude, G minor

494 BRAHMS Waltz, Op 39, No. 8

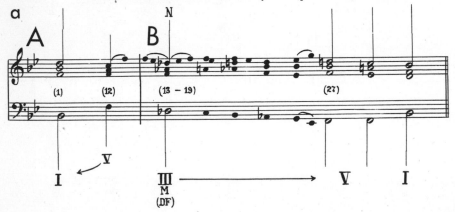

493 cont'd

a cont'd

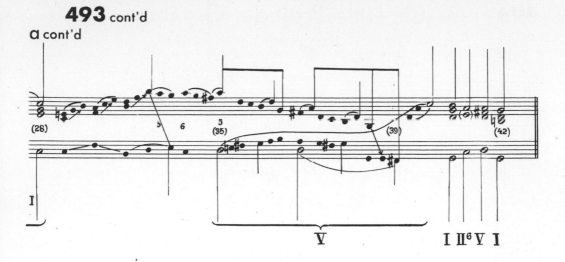

495

a

BACH Minuet 2 (Partita No. 1)

496

a

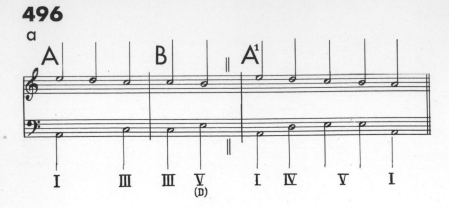

I   III   III   V   I   IV   V   I
                    (D)

497 SCHUBERT Symphony, B minor.
1st movement

a

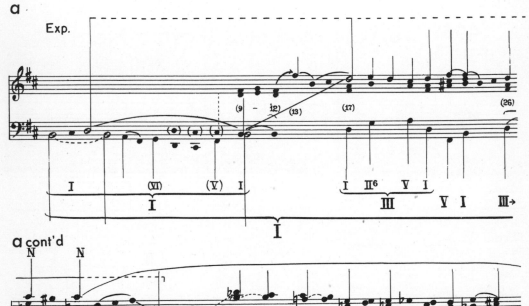

a cont'd

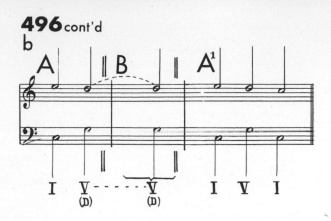

496 cont'd

497 cont'd

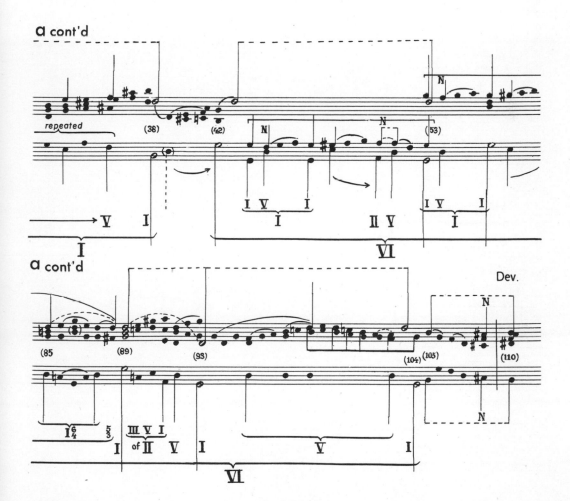

a cont'd

Dev.

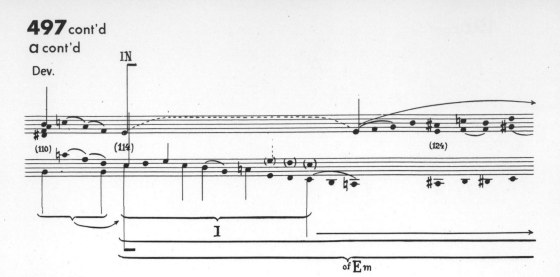

a cont'd

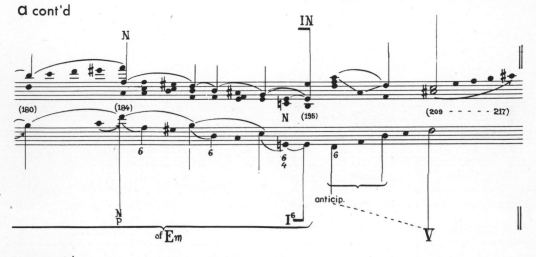

a cont'd

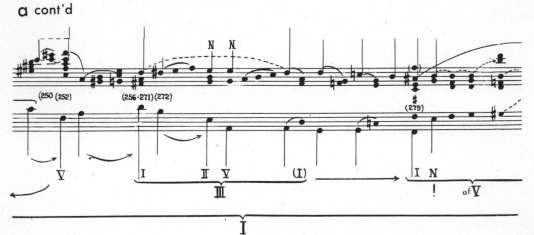

a cont'd

a cont'd

Rec.

a cont'd

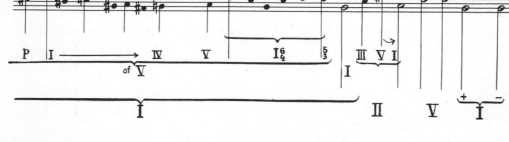

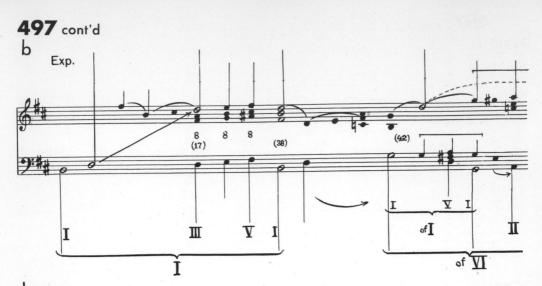

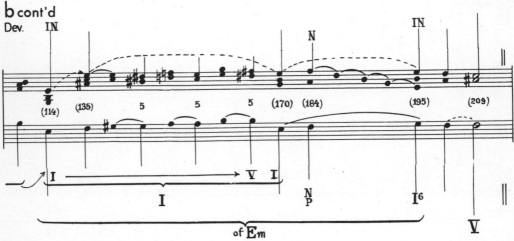

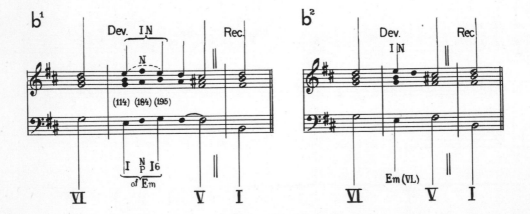

b cont'd

b cont'd
Rec.

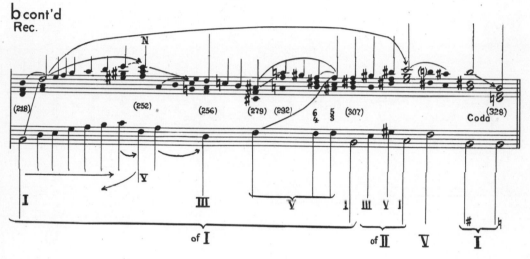

c

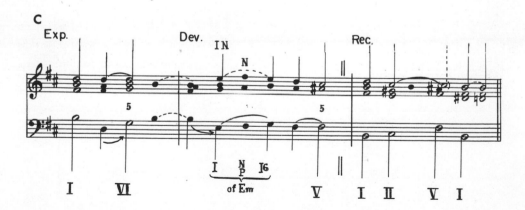

RAVEL Sonatina. 1st movement

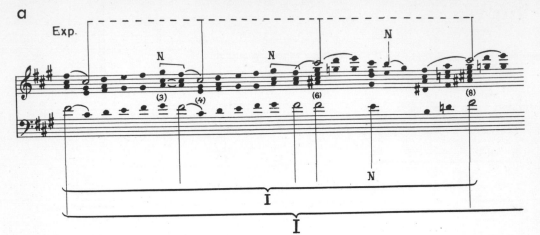

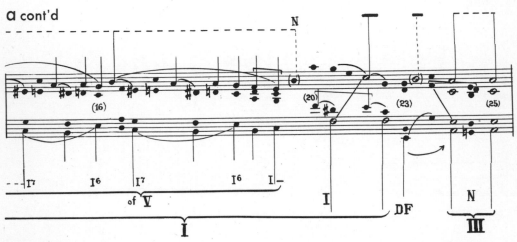

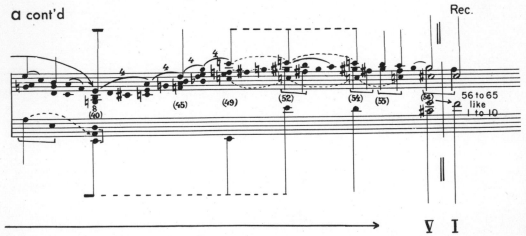

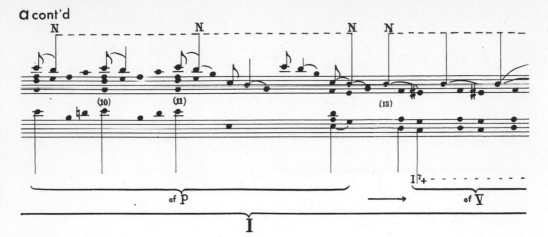

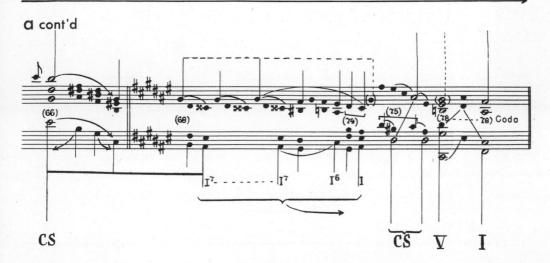

498 cont'd

b

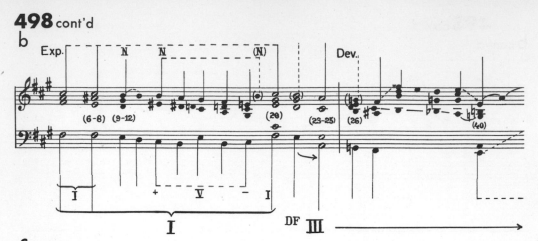

c

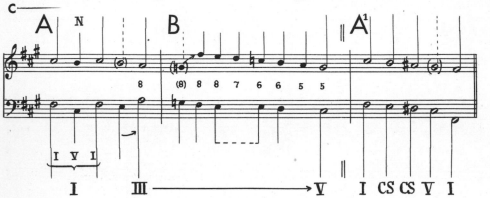

500 CHOPIN Nocturne, Op 9, No. 2

a .

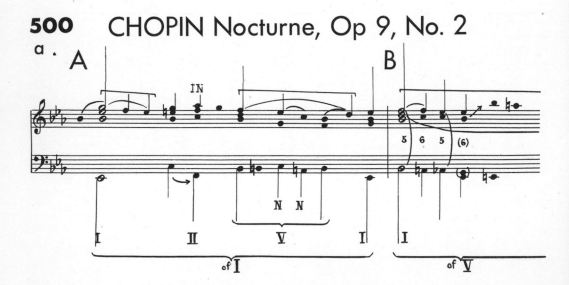

498 cont'd

b cont'd

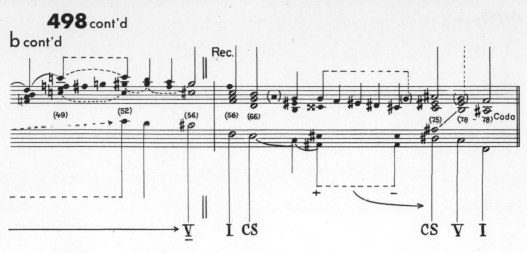

499 CHOPIN Mazurka, Op 17, No. 2

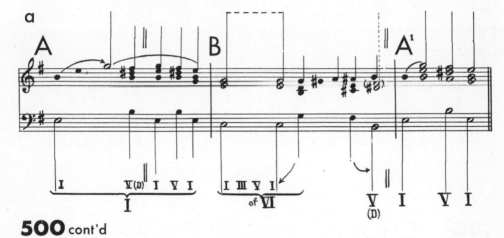

500 cont'd

a cont'd

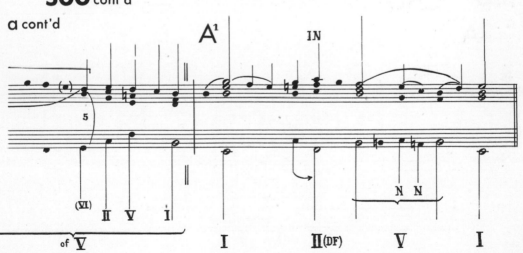

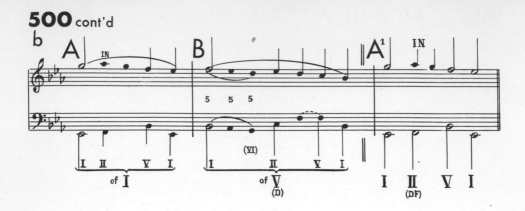

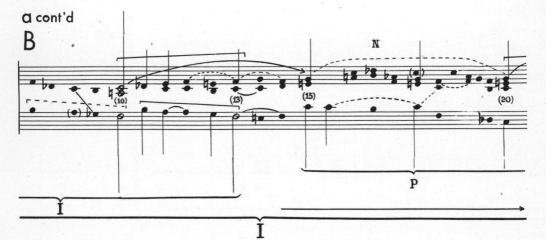

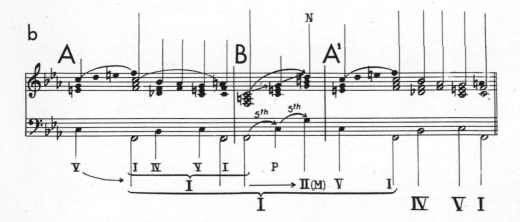

MONTEVERDI Madrigal:
Lasciatemi morire

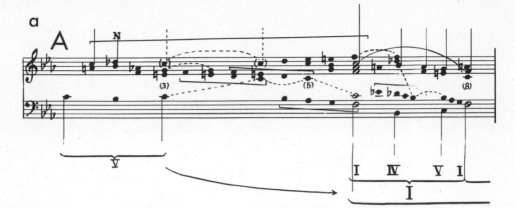

a

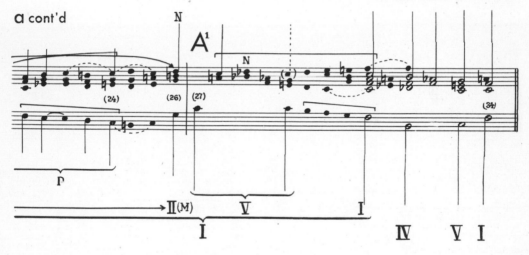

a cont'd

c

a

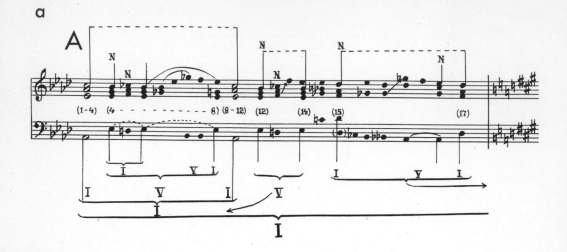

a cont'd

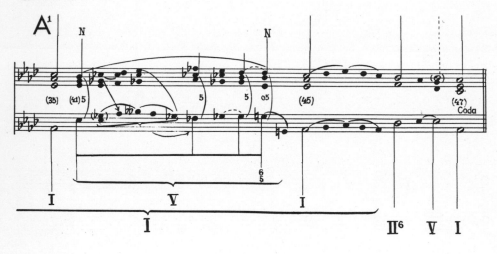

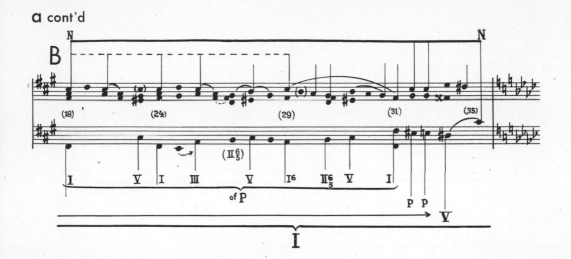

a cont'd

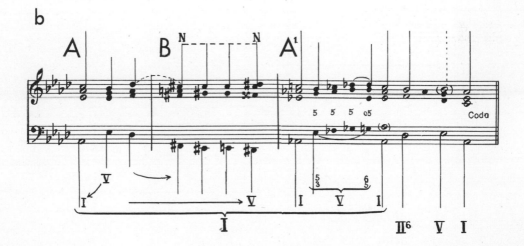

b

503 **BRAHMS Symphony No. 3.**
1st movement

a

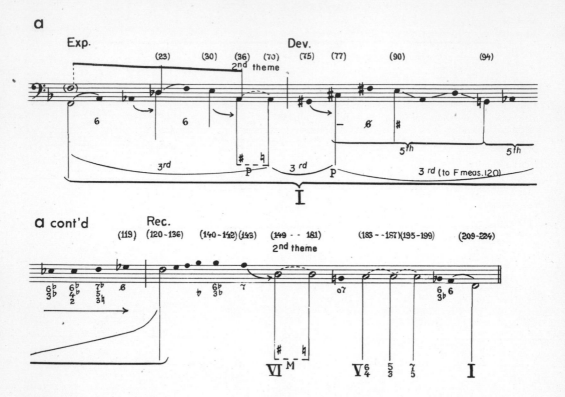

504 **BARTÓK Bourrée (Mikrokosmos, Bk IV)**

a

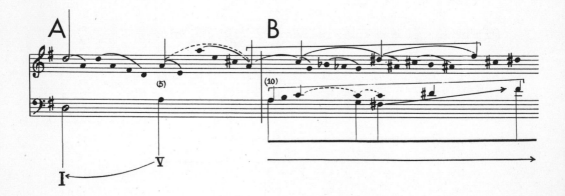

a cont'd

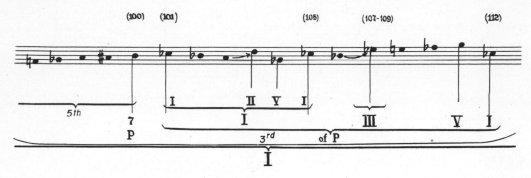

b

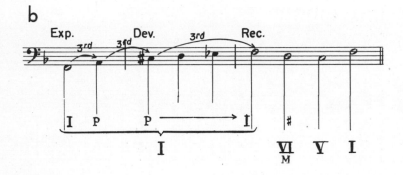

a cont'd

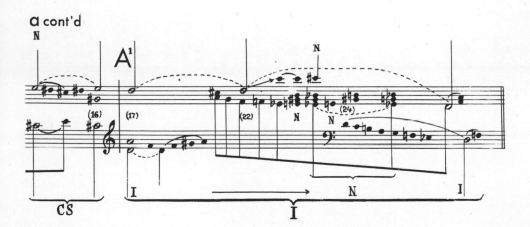

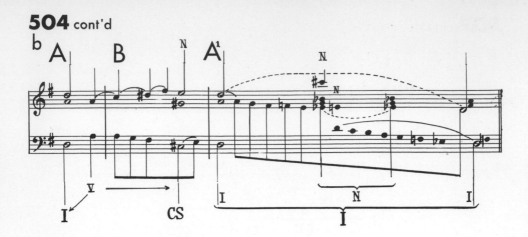

505 HINDEMITH Piano Sonata No. 2
1st movement

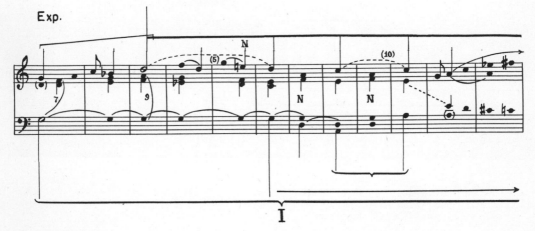

504 cont'd

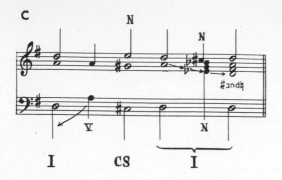

505 cont'd

a cont'd

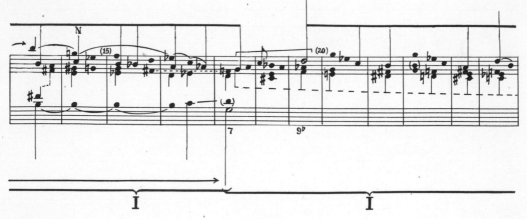

a cont'd

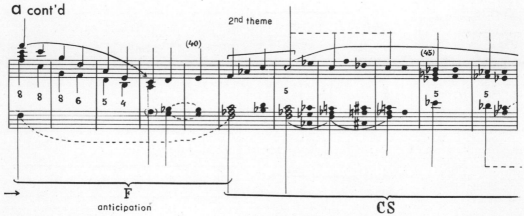

a cont'd

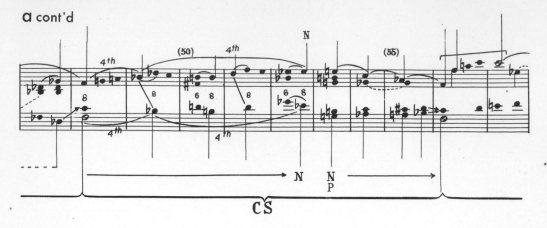

a cont'd

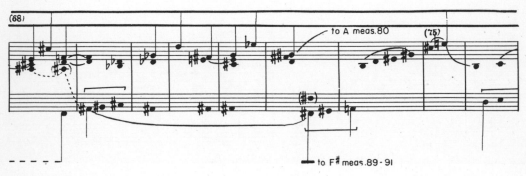

a cont'd

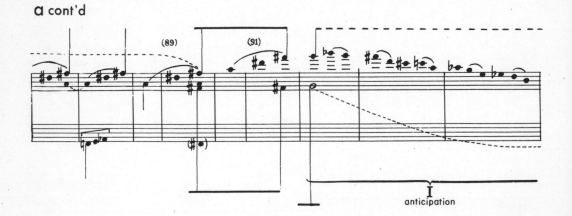

a cont'd

Dev.

via F# to G (meas. 95)

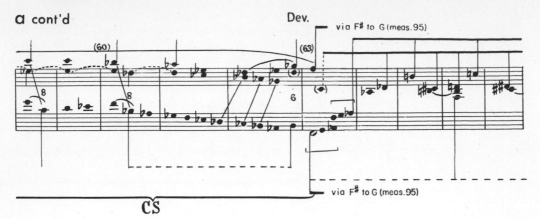

CS

a cont'd

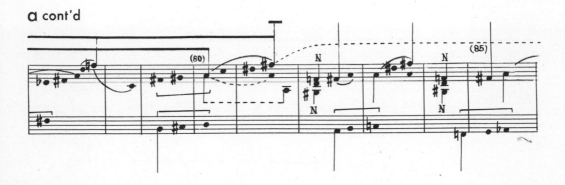

a cont'd
Rec.

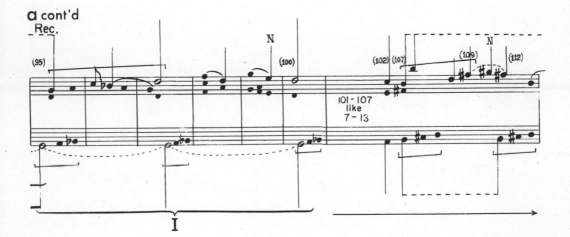

101-107
like
7-13

I

a cont'd

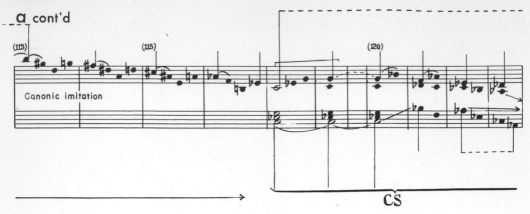

a cont'd

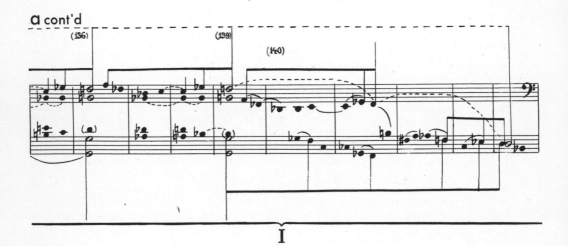

b

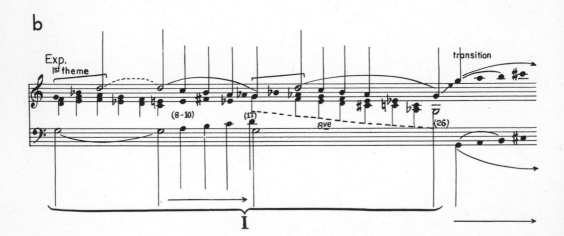

a cont'd

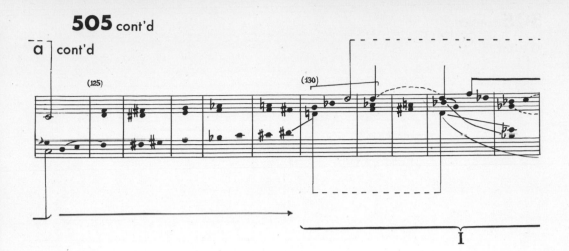

a cont'd

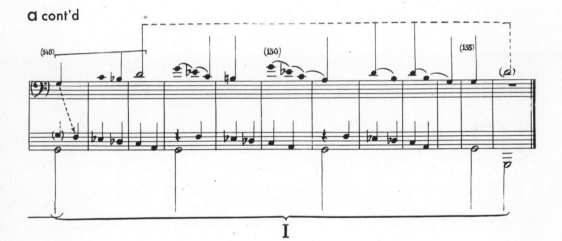

b cont'd

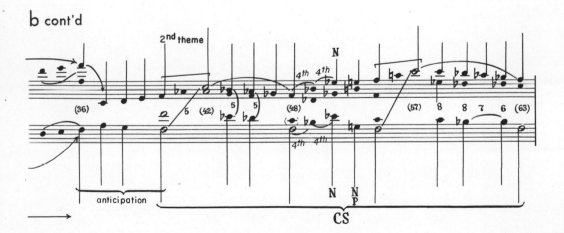

b cont'd
Dev.

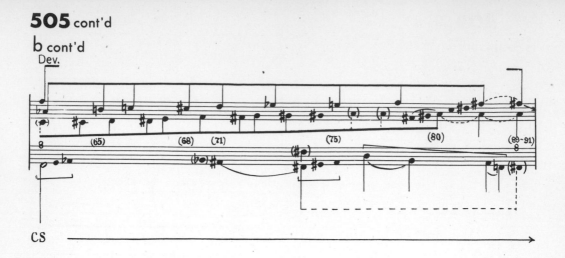

CS

c

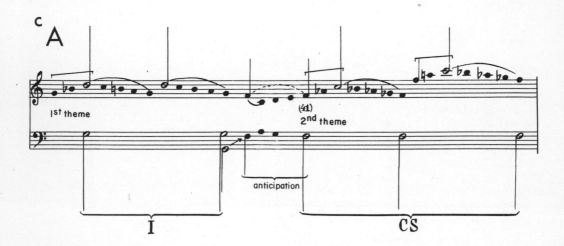

d

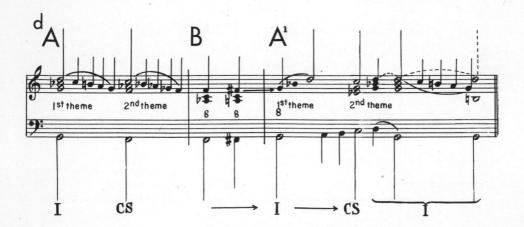

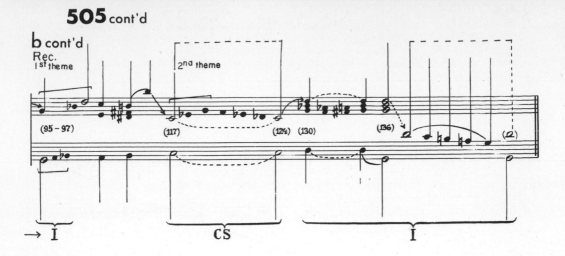

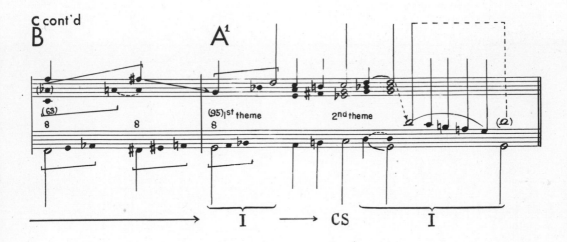

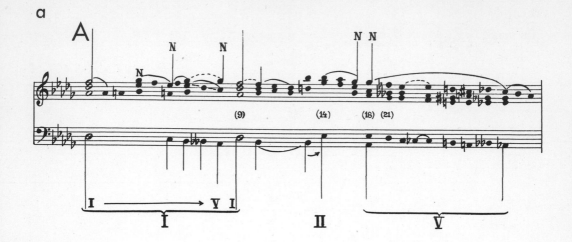

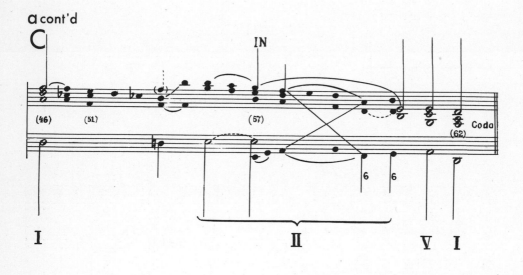

a cont'd

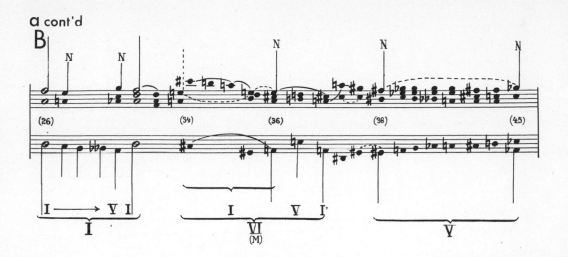

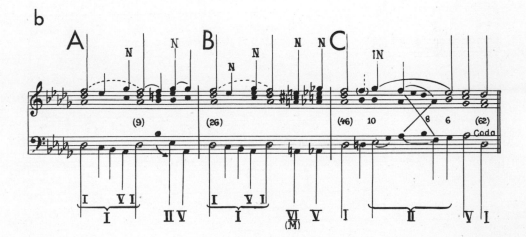

507 ## MOZART Fantasia, C minor, K. 475

a
Adagio

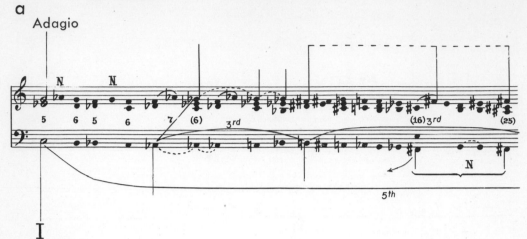

a cont'd
Allegro

a cont'd
Andantino

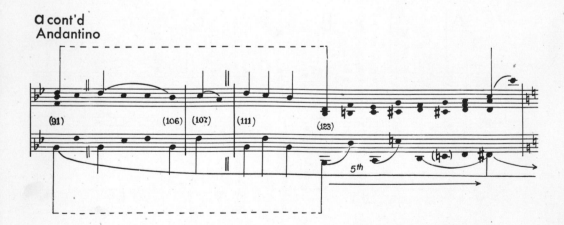

308

a cont'd

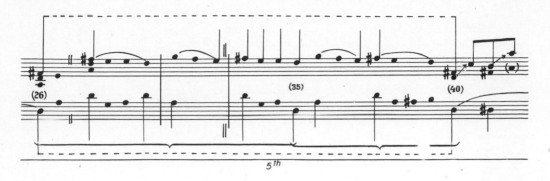

a cont'd

a cont'd
Più Allegro
to A♭ meas. 143

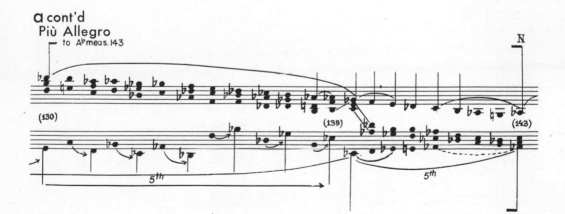

a cont'd

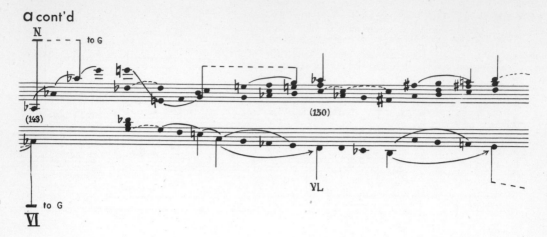

b

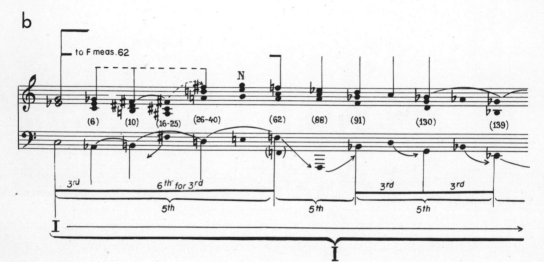

c

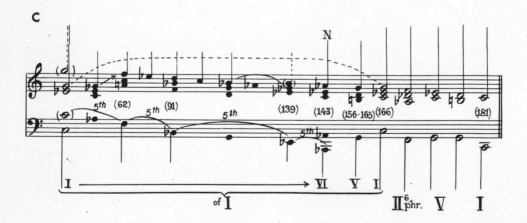

a cont'd

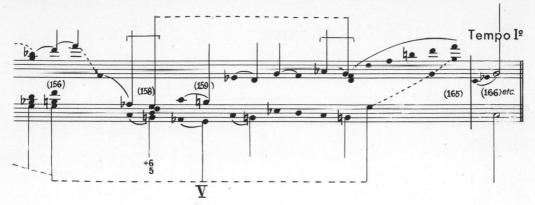

b cont'd

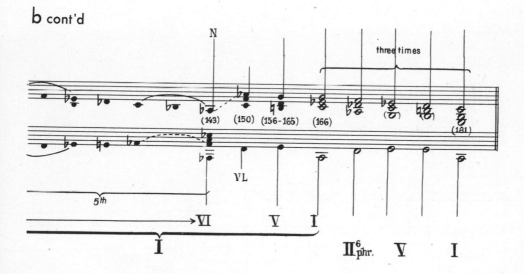

508 CHOPIN Nocturne, Op 37, No. 2

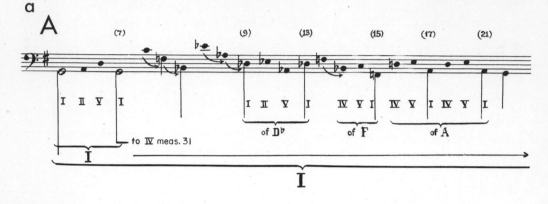

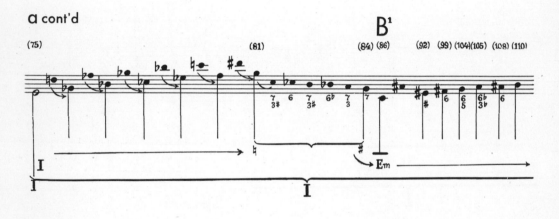

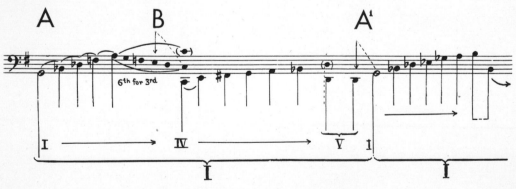

508 cont'd

a cont'd

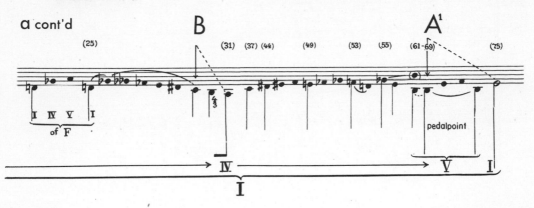

a cont'd

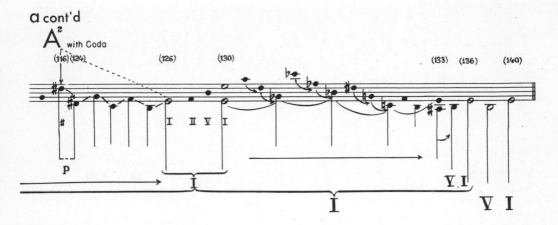

b cont'd

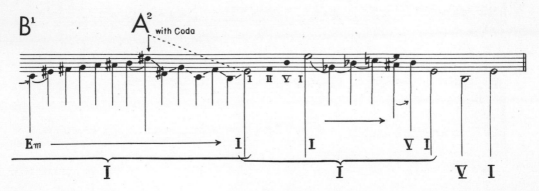

509 LASSO Christe Dei soboles

Chri - ste, de-i so-bo-les, spes ___ et ___ me - a so-

la vo - lu - ptas, etc.

etc.

[From *HDM*, Vol. I, P. 333]

Part III Chapter Two

510 ALLELUIA ANGELUS DOMINI

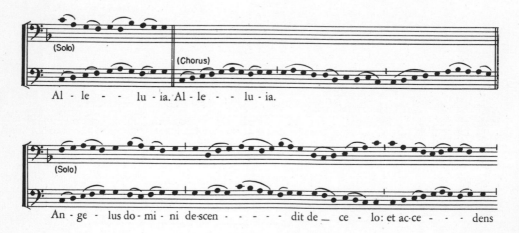

(Solo) (Chorus)

Al - le - - lu - ia. Al - le - - lu - ia.

(Solo)

An - ge - lus do - mi - ni de-scen - - - - - dit de _ ce - lo: et ac-ce - - - dens

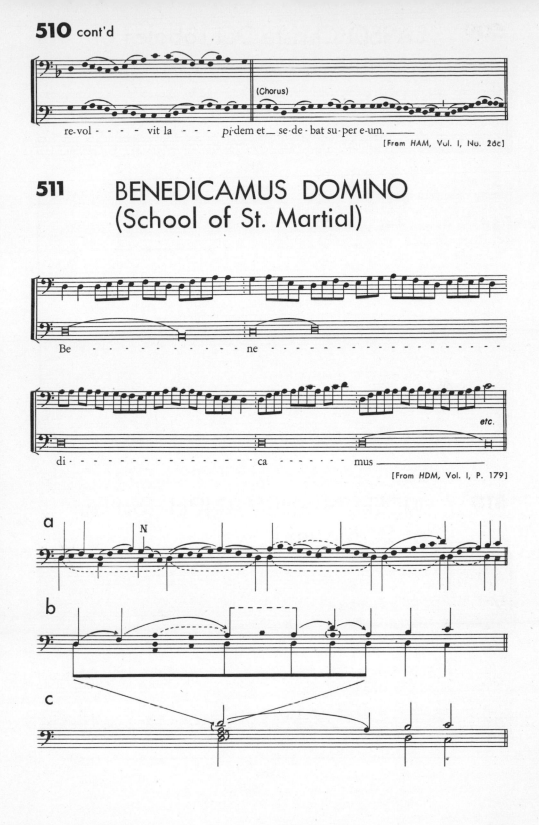

re-vol - - - - vit la - - - pi-dem et __ se-de - bat su-per e-um. __

[From HAM, Vol. I, No. 26c]

511 # BENEDICAMUS DOMINO
(School of St. Martial)

Be - - - - - - - - - - - ne

di - - - - - - - - - - - - ca - - - - - mus __ *etc.*

[From HDM, Vol. I, P. 179]

a   N

b

c

512 BENEDICAT ERGO (School of Compostela)

Be - ne - di - cat er - go plebs fi - de - - lis

do - mi - no

[From *HDM*, Vol. I, P. 182]

a

a cont'd

513 VIDERUNT HEMANUEL (School of St. Martial)

Vi - de - runt _____ He - - ma - nu - - - - - el

[From *HAM*, Vol. I, No. 27a]

a

C?

G

Alleluia, etc.

(5)

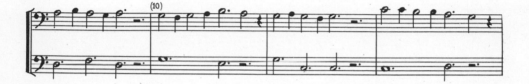

(10)

(15)

(20)

[From AUDM, PP. 94-95]

a

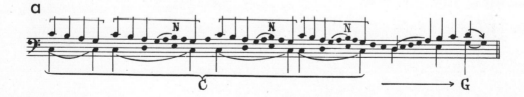

ORGANUM (Style of Perotinus)

[From *HAM*, Vol. I, No. 31]

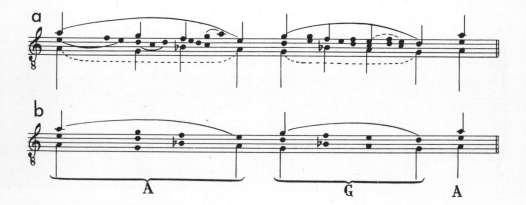

516   ## PEROTINUS Organum Triplum

[From *HDM*, Vol. I, P. 226]

516 cont'd

a

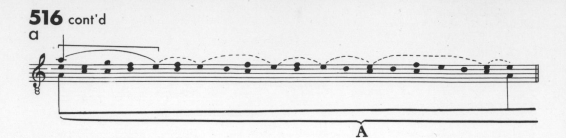

A

a cont'd

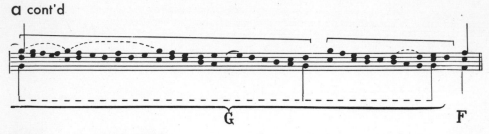

G   F

517   MOTET

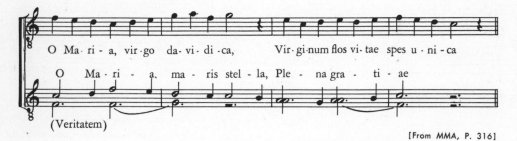

O Ma - ri - a, vir - go da - vi - di - ca,   Vir - gi - num flos vi - tae spes u - ni - ca

O   Ma - ri - a,   ma - ris stel - la, Ple - - na gra - ti - ae

(Veritatem)

[From *MMA*, P. 316]

a

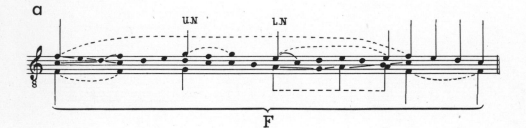

U.N   L.N

F

b

F

a cont'd

A

N

b

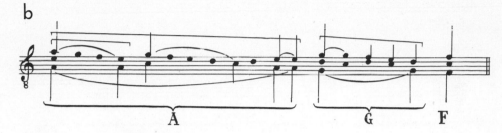

A   G   F

518   MOTET

Quant flou - rist la vi - o - le - te, La rose et la flour de glay,

Non _____ or - pha - num te de - se - ram. Sed ef - fe - ram

Et gaudebit.

[From CM, No. 67]

a

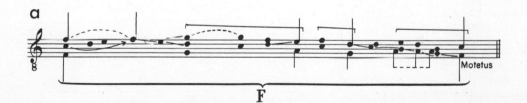

F

Motetus

b

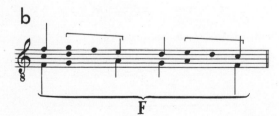

F

c

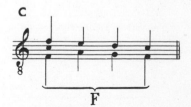

F

519   MOTET

Sed ho-mi--num in-ter tot mi-li-a

Qui to-ci--us vi-res in-ge-ni-i

(Egregie)

[From CM, No. 79]

a

A

b   Motetus   Triplum   Motetus   both

A

520   MOTET

Qui a-mours vuelt main-te-nir Et — ser-vir Lo-iau--ment sans faus-

Li dous pen--ser — Qui mi vient de ce li

Cis a cui je sui a-mi-e Est

ser, Biense_ doit sour tou-te riens gar--der

Que J'aim de cuer,— Car tous jours l'ai ser--vi Sans gui-

preux — et gais, Pour s'a-mour se-

De vi - la - ni - e, Qui __ tant fait a blas - - mer,

ler, Et bons es - - poirs que j'ai d'avoir

rai jo - li - e Tant com vi - vrai.

[From CM, No. 54]

a

b

Melodic outline

521 MOTET

O Ma - ri - - a, re - gi - na __ glo - ri - - -

Au - di, Pa - ter, sal - va nos, tu qui

Alleluya

e, Fons in - dul - - gen - ci - - e, Tu - - um, Ma -

es Sa - lus et __ re - qui - - es Et re - ple __

521 cont'd

ter, ex - o - ra ____ Fi - li - um, Ut pro no - -

nos spi - ri - tu di - vi - no, Ut ____ gra - ci -

a

b

522 MOTET

L'au - tre jour par un ma - - - ti - net M'en a - -

Hier ____ ma - ti - net Trou - vai sans son

Omnes,

lai - es be - ni - ant Et trou-vai sans son ber - ge - ret

ber - ge - ret Pas - toure es - ga - re - - - e;

[From CM, No. 40]

521 cont'd

bis ex - o - - - ret ____ Do - mi - - - - - num.

as a - ga - - mus ____ Do - mi - - - - - no.

ɑ cont'd

[From CM, No. 9]

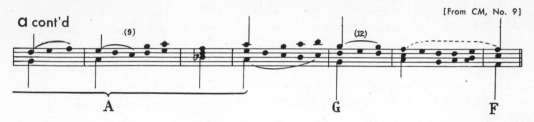

A ⟶ G ⟶ F

522 cont'd

ɑ

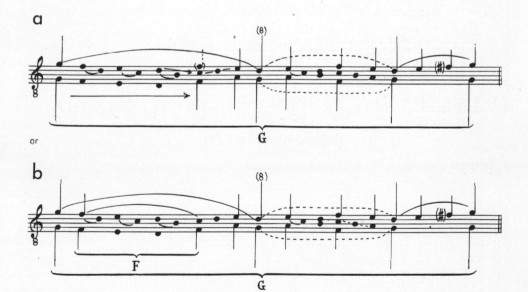

G

or

b

F

G

523 RONDEAU: Amours et ma dame aussi

A-mours et ma dame aus - si jointes mains vous proi mer - chi!
etc.

[From MMA, P. 322]

a

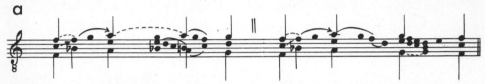

524 ADAM DE LA HALLE Li maus d'amer (1st part)

Li maus d'a - - - mer me plaist miex a sen - - - - tir

K'a main-ta - mant ne fait li dons de joi - e, etc.

[From HAM, Vol. I, No. 36a]

525 ADAM DE LA HALLE Rondeau: Tant con je vivrai

Tant con je vi - - - vrai N'a - me - - - -

525 cont'd

rai au - - - - - - - - trui que _____ vous. etc.

[From HAM, Vol. I, No. 36b]

a

526 MOTET

Entre, etc.

Chief, etc.

Aptatur

[From CM, No. 24]

a

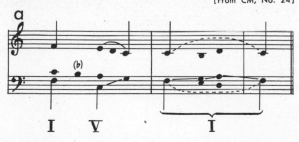

I   V   I

527 MOTET

Au dous, etc.

Biaus, etc.

Manere

[From CM, No. 18]

528 MACHAUT Virelai (No. 38)

De _ tout _ sui si con-for - - te-e

[From MW, Vol. I]

529 MACHAUT Virelai (No. 32)

Da - me mon _ cuer em - por - - tes

[From MW, Vol. I]

530 ## MACHAUT Ballade (No. 3)

(flour etc.)

[From MW, Vol. I]

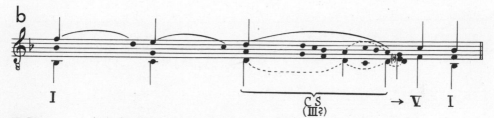

a

b

I   C S   → V   I
(III?)

531 ## MACHAUT Rondeau (No. 13)

Da - me, — se — vous n'a - vez a - per - ce - u

que ————— je vous aim de ——— cuer, etc.

[From MW, Vol. I]

a

b

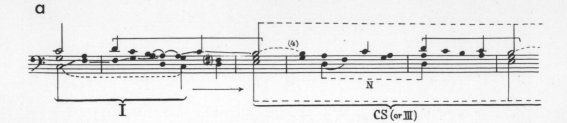

532   MACHAUT Virelai (No. 31)

1.5 Plus du - - re que un dy - a - mant   ne que __ pier - re d'a - y -
4. par un __ ac - cueil __ at - trai - - ant,   m'ont au __ cuer en __ re - - sgar -

mant est __ vo dur - - té,   da - me qui __ n'a - ves pi - - té, de
dant si __ fort na - - vré   que ja - mais __ joi - e n'a - - vré, ju - -

a cont'd

CS(or III)

vostre a - -mant   qu'o ci - - -es en _ de - - si - rant vostre _ a - mi - tié.
sques a - -tant   que vo _ gra-ce _ quïl a - tant m'au - res don - né.

2. Dá - me, _ vo pu - - re _ biau - té   qui _ tou - tes _ passe,_
3. simple et _ plein d'u _ mi - li - té,   de _ dou-ceur _ fi - -

a _ mon-gré, et _ vo _ sam-blant   ne _ pa -   ré, en _ sous-ri - - - ant,

[From MW, Vol. I]

331

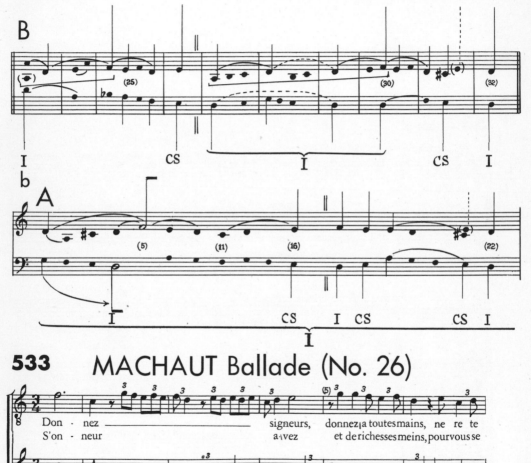

533 MACHAUT Ballade (No. 26)

Don - nez _____ signeurs, donnez a toutes mains, ne re te

S'on - neur a vez et de richesses meins, pour vous se

a cont'd

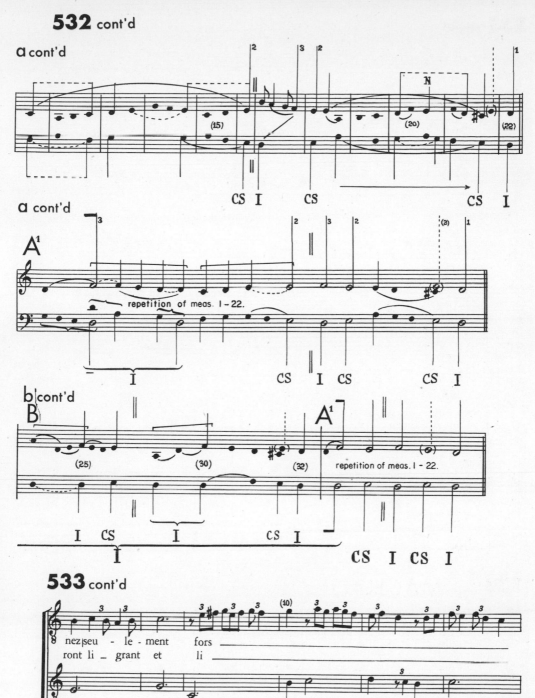

a cont'd

repetition of meas. 1 – 22.

b cont'd

(25) (30) (32) repetition of meas. 1 - 22.

533 cont'd

nez seu – le – ment fors

ront li – grant et li

l'on - neur.

me - neur

cha - scuns ___ di - -

ra: ___ ci a vaillant si·gneur. Et terre aus-siqu'est despen . . . . . du . . . . . . e

a

A

(3)   (6)   N   (9)

a cont'd

B

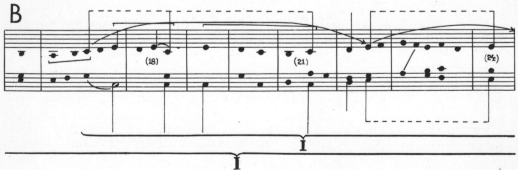

(18)   (21)   (24)

I

I

vaut trop mieus que ter - - re per - du - - - - - - - - - - - e

[From MW, Vol. I]

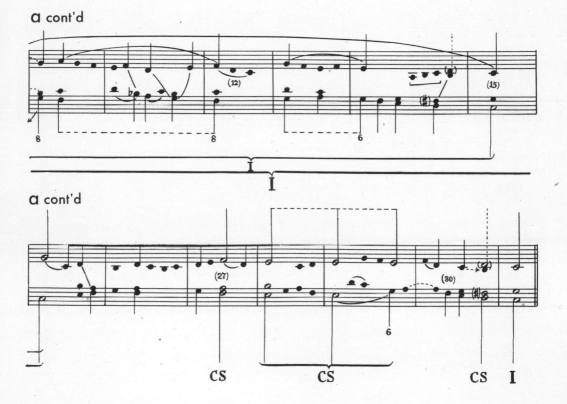

533 cont'd

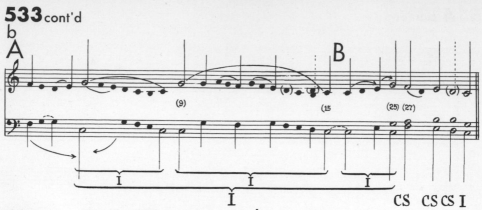

(9)   (15)   (25) (27)

CS CS CS I

534 ## DUNSTABLE Sub tuam protectionem

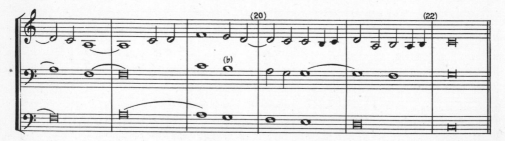

[From *TC*, Vol. I, P. 198]

534 cont'd

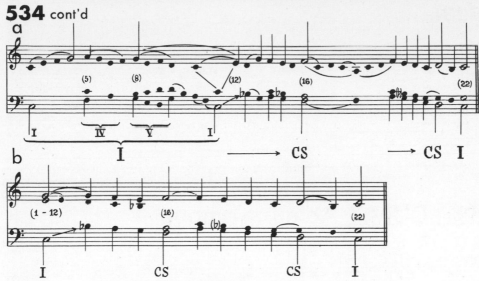

535 DUNSTABLE Puisque m'amour

Puis-que m'a_ mour m'a_ pris en _____ des _____ plai-

sir

[From *TC*, Vol. I, P. 254]

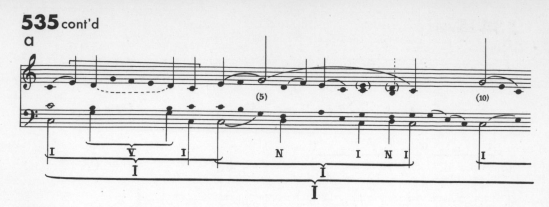

536   DUFAY Adieu m'amour

A — — — dieu m'a — mour, a — — dieu — ma ioy — — —

A - dieu — — m'a - mour, a - -dieu — ma ioy — — — —

e, A - dieu le so - las que i'a - voy — — — —

e, A - dieu le so - las que i'a - voy — — — — — — —

— (#) — e, A - dieu ma — le - a - le mais tres — — — se.

— — — e, — A - dieu ma — le - a - le mais tres — — — — — se.

a cont'd

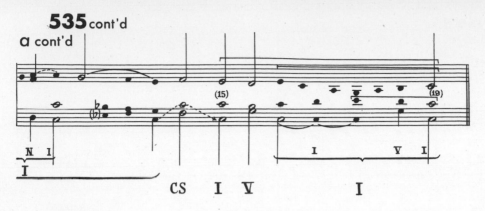

536 cont'd

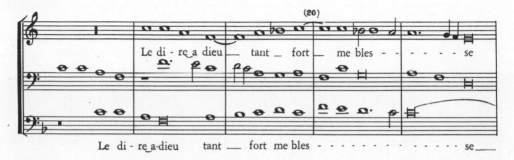

Le di - re a dieu ___ tant ___ fort ___ me bles - - - - se

Le di - re a-dieu tant ___ fort me bles - - - - - - - - - se ___

Qu'il me sam - ble que mo - rir doy -

Qu'il me sam - ble que mo - rir doy - - - -

e

e.

[From *DAS CHORWERK*, Vol. XIX]

a

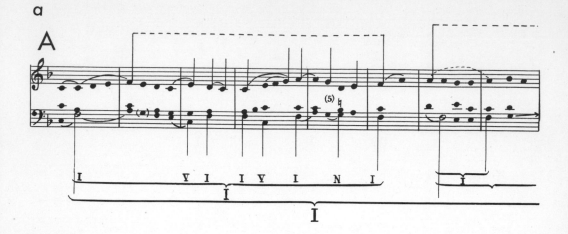

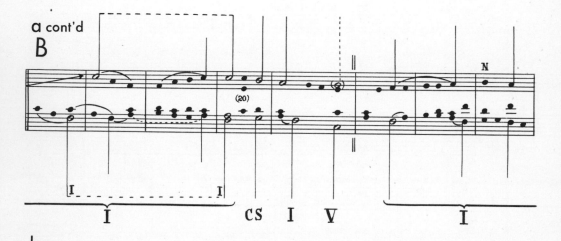

b

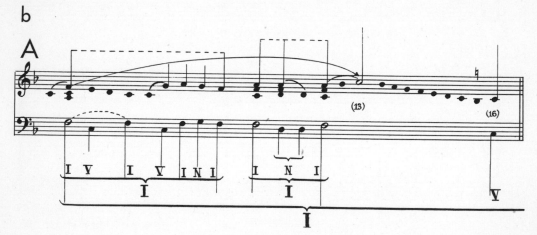

a cont'd

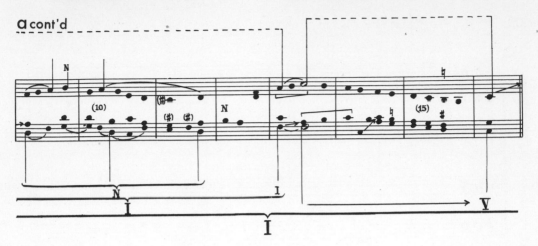

a cont'd

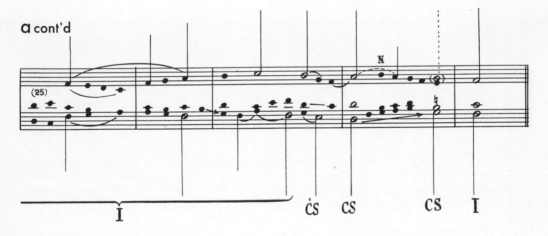

b cont'd

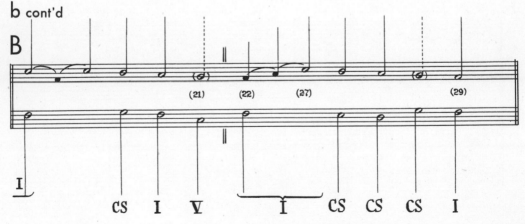

537 OBRECHT Osanna (Missa: Je ne demande)

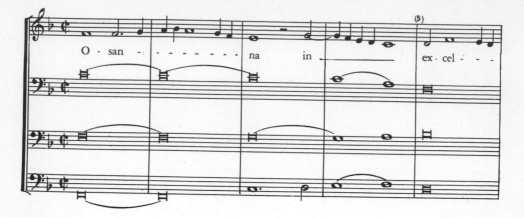

O - san - - - - - - - - - - na in _____ ex - cel - - - -

- - - - - - - - - sis, etc.

[From *WJO, Missen,* Vol. I, No. 1]

a

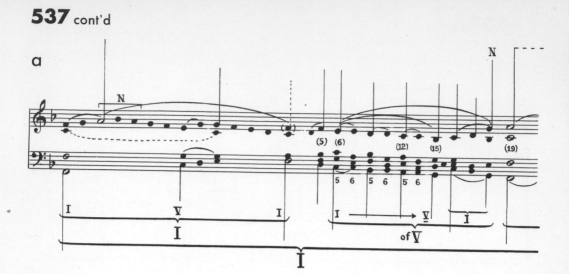

b

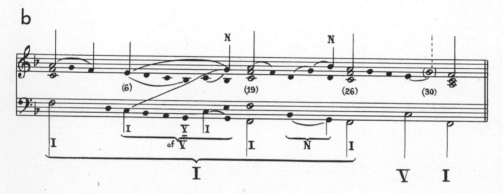

538   ISAAC Kyrie (Missa Carminum)

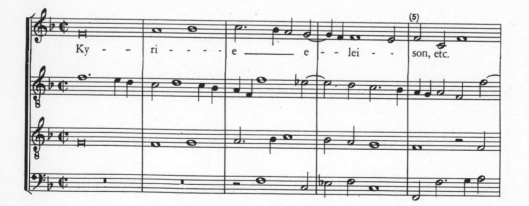

Ky - ri - - - e _ e - lei - - son, etc.

a cont'd

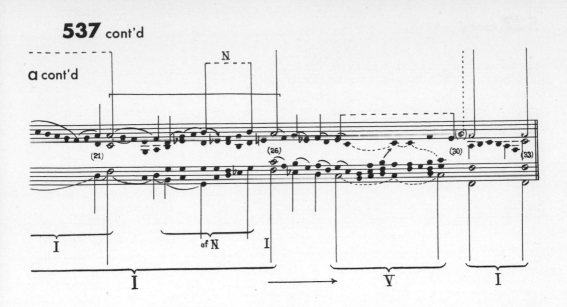

[From DAS CHORWERK, Vol. VII]

a

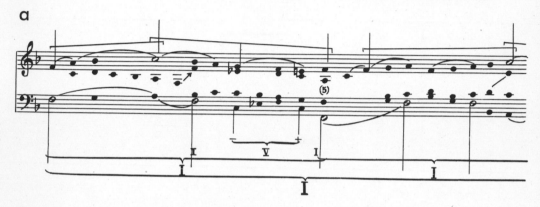

539 JOSQUIN Motet: O Domine Jesu Christe (1st part)

a cont'd

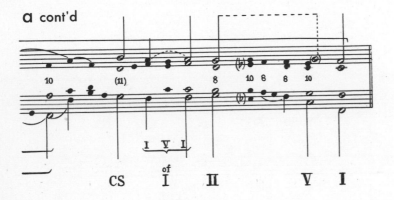

CS   I   II   V   I

539 cont'd

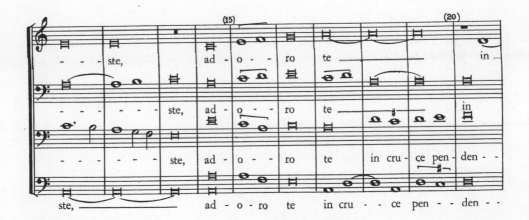

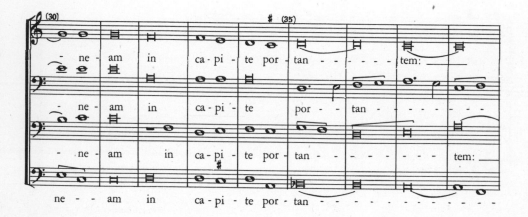

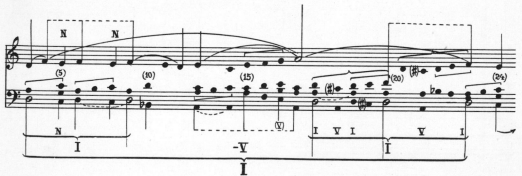

de - - pre- cor - te, ut i -psa crux li - be - -ret
tem: __ de - - pre- cor - - te, ut i -psa crux li - be - -ret
__ de - - pre- cor __ te, ut i -psa crux li -be -ret
tem: de - - - pre- cor __ te, ut i -psa crux li -be - -ret

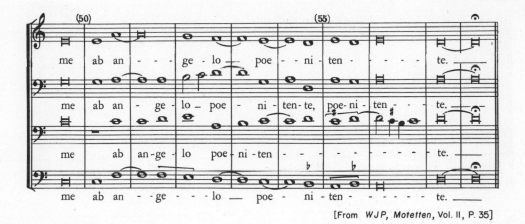

me ab an - - - ge- lo __ poe - - ni -ten - - - - te.
me ab an - ge- lo- poe - ni -ten- te, poe- ni - ten - - te.
me ab an -ge- lo poe - ni -ten - - - - - te.
me ab an - ge - - lo __ poe - ni -ten - - - - - te.

[From *WJP*, *Motetten*, Vol. II, P. 35]

a cont'd

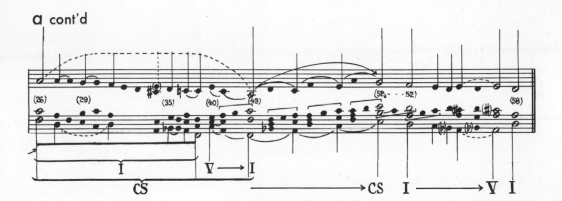